NYMANS

THE STORY OF A SUSSEX GARDEN

Ludwig Messel in his garden at Nymans *c.* 1910. The house is just visible behind the monkey-puzzle tree

NYMANS

THE STORY OF A SUSSEX GARDEN

SHIRLEY NICHOLSON

SUTTON PUBLISHING
In Association with the National Trust

Published in Association with the National Trust
First published in the United Kingdom in 1992 by
Sutton Publishing · Phoenix Mill · Stroud · Gloucestershire

British Library Cataloguing in Publication Data

A catalogue record for this book is available from the British Library.

ISBN 0-7509-2872-7

Typeset in 11/13 Bembo.
Typesetting and origination by
Sutton Publishing Limited.
Printed and bound in England by
J.H. Haynes & Co. Ltd, Sparkford.

Contents

Acknowledgements

M y sincere thanks to Anne, Countess of Rosse, whose campaign for the appreciation of our Victorian heritage was the inspiration behind my first book, *A Victorian Household*, based on the diaries of her maternal grandparents, Marion and Linley Sambourne. This second book, concerning her Messel forebears and their garden at Nymans, owes a debt to her also.

I am very grateful to the members of the Messel family who have been so helpful and encouraging over the last three years. Victoria Allison (née Messel) urged me to make a start and has painted the flowers which are special to Nymans; Judith Hiller provided information about the family's early years in Darmstadt and London; Thomas Messel, Mary Parker, Anne Renshaw, Lord Rosse, Lord Snowdon and Anthony Weiler all told me something about the middle period; Alistair Buchanan discussed the present and looked into the future. Everyone joined in the search for illustrations and a selection from old family albums adds interest to the story.

I am indebted to the National Trust staff at Polesden Lacey for allowing access to their archive on Nymans. John Sales, Gardens Adviser to the Trust, and Graham Stuart Thomas kindly spared time for helpful discussions; David Masters, Head Gardener at Nymans, spent many hours answering questions and showing me around the garden. These opportunities to learn more about rare plants and the management of a large estate were greatly appreciated.

Last but not least, my thanks to the Royal Horticultural Society for the use of their splendid Lindley Library, a treasure-house for which all gardeners must be forever grateful.

Photographs and Illustrations

The author and publishers would like to thank the following for permission to reproduce photographs and illustrations:

Peter Barratt/National Trust 162; C. Renow-Clarke/National Trust 160; Tony Cook/National Trust plate 2; *Country Life* 70, 71; the *Evening Argus* 157; John Hardy 134; David Masters/National Trust 146,

159, 167, plates 3, 4, 6, 12; Victoria Messel (flower paintings) plates 8a–d, 14a–d, 15a–d; the *Mid-Sussex Times* 155; National Trust Photographic Library/Nick Meers plates 7, 9, 10, 16; David Nicholson, 90, plates 5, 17; Reed International Books (Alfred Parsons' drawings) xi, 17, 51, 74, 88, 142, 166; Mark Roylance/National Trust plate 11; the Earl of Rosse 91; Snowdon 120, 127, 152; Cliff Towler 164; the Victorian Society (photographs at Linley Sambourne House/Royal Borough of Kensington and Chelsea) 34, 56, 129; Steven Wooster plates 1, 13.

All other illustrations have come from the Messel family albums with their kind permission.

Note

Most of the gardens mentioned in the book are open to the public during the summer months, but it is advisable to check times before visiting. Nymans, Wakehurst Place and Sheffield Park belong to the National Trust; Leonardslee, The High Beeches and Borde Hill are privately owned; Gravetye Manor and South Lodge are now hotels. Compton's Brow has been absorbed into a housing estate.

Introduction

This is the story of the garden at Nymans in Sussex, owned for over sixty years by the Messel family and since 1953 the property of the National Trust. Three strands are interwoven in the tale: the first concerns the several members of the family and their staff who created and maintained the garden, the second is the history of plant introductions over the last hundred years and the third is the modern enthusiasm for the preservation and restoration of historic gardens and landscapes.

Much has been written recently about Edwardian gardens. The partnership of Gertrude Jekyll and Edwin Lutyens, who skilfully combined architectural elements with lavish 'cottage garden' planting, is especially well known, but during the same period English gardens were being transformed in other, broader, ways. Parkland well furnished with exotic trees and flowering shrubs – especially rhododendrons – was considered a more exciting option by many estate owners and the development of Nymans in the years before the First World War is closely paralleled by that of several other properties nearby, where the rich acid soil and sheltered valleys of the Sussex Weald provided ideal conditions for experimentation.

Nymans is now open to the public and many thousands of people come every year to enjoy a varied and richly planted garden in a beautiful rural setting. Both could be described as typically English, but, like so many other good things in this country, the garden at Nymans owes its genesis to a foreigner. Many of our most famous artists, scientists, financiers and politicians have been immigrants, attracted by the opportunities for a better life that England offered. Gardening, in which art and science are united, is a discipline at which the English are reckoned to excel, yet even here the debt to other countries has been immense.

Ludwig Messel, who purchased Nymans in 1890, was of German origin. Well educated and of good family, he came to London in the late 1860s. Here he founded a successful stockbroking firm, married an English girl and raised six children. In middle age he bought a country house and took up gardening as a hobby. His rapidly growing enthusiasm coincided with a great influx of new plants from the far corners of the world: trees, flowering shrubs, herbaceous plants and bulbs, all hitherto unknown in Europe, wrought a fundamental change in the way landscapes were designed and planted. Today most of the best plants in our gardens are foreigners, yet so quickly have they become assimilated that it is difficult to imagine the English scene without them. The Messel family too were rapidly absorbed into the life of their adopted country: Ludwig's sons served with distinction in the First World War; his grandson Oliver became a stage-designer, greatly admired on both sides of the Atlantic; and his great grandson, Antony Armstrong-Jones, married into the royal family.

Ludwig Messel died in 1915, but his son Leonard continued to enlarge the stock of unusual plants at Nymans and under his care several valuable new hybrids were raised. The 1920s and 1930s were the heyday of the 'Sussex style' and Nymans became a recognised place of pilgrimage for all keen horticulturists. Financial restraints after the Second World War brought this golden age to a halt and when it became clear that no descendant could afford to keep up the garden unaided, Leonard Messel bequeathed the whole property to the National Trust. But family interest remained unbroken as Leonard's daughter Anne was made Director of the garden. She and her husband Michael, sixth Earl of Rosse, were both dedicated and knowledgeable gardeners and they shared the decision-making at Nymans with the Trust's advisers for the next quarter of a century.

Any alteration at Nymans was resisted during that period, but the problems of continuity versus new ideas (always present in a gardener's mind) are especially acute for the National Trust, which places great emphasis on the historical importance of properties in its care. The great storm of October 1987, in which so many gardens suffered terrible damage, forced the Trust to reconsider its priorities. At Nymans nearly all the fine old trees were lost, as well as many valuable shrubs. The ruin of so much love and care was daunting, and for a time it seemed as if recovery would be impossible. Fortunately the Trust was able to allocate funds for a major replanting scheme, and already the scars are healing. The redesigned Pinetum is showing promise, the Laurel Walk and special groupings of historic plants are growing well, while the Rose Garden – now less shaded than of old – has never looked better. Ludwig Messel, should he return today, would have no difficulty in recognising his creation; the epithets 'instructive' and 'beautiful' used by his friend William Robinson in 1917 are still applicable. Restored and refurbished, Nymans is set to delight its visitors for another century.

Cornus nuttalli

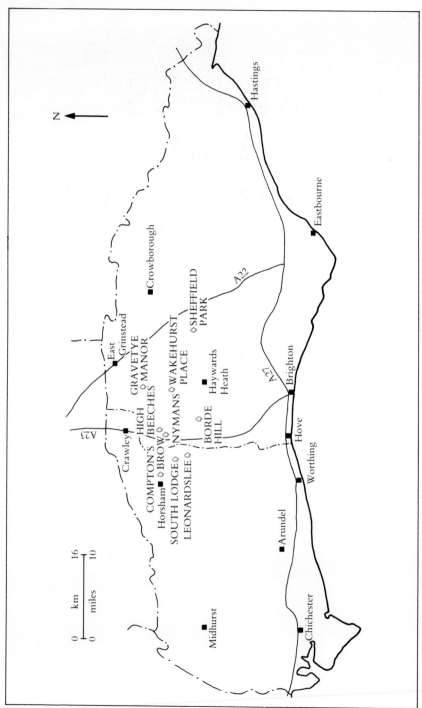

Map of Sussex, showing some of the gardens which were being developed at the same time as Nymans

Part I

NYMANS
AND
LUDWIG MESSEL

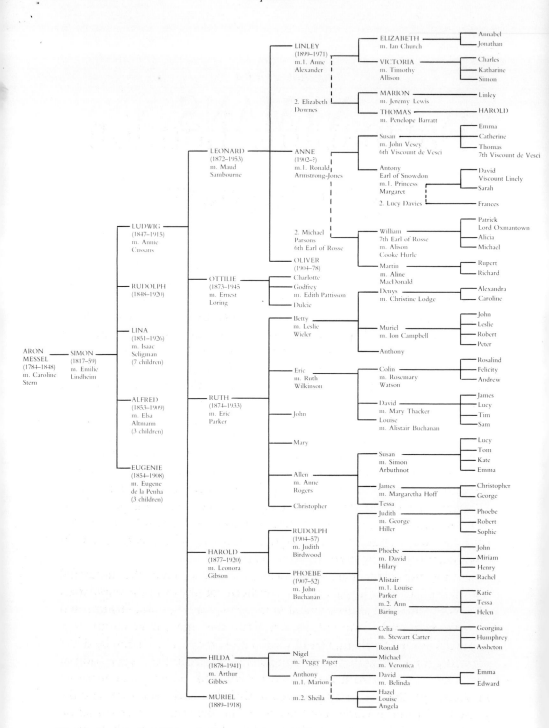

The Messel family tree (those born a Messel in capital letters)

Chapter One

Darmstadt, London and Sussex

Nymans lies five miles south of Crawley in Sussex, on the outskirts of Handcross, a village now bypassed by the main London to Brighton road. The house and its surrounding estate is said to take its unusual name from Robert Nyuweman, who is known to have held land in this part of the county during the fourteenth century. Details of ownership before the eighteenth century are scanty, but Gerald Gatland possessed 89 acres of land here in 1597 and a 'mansion house' belonging to Gerard Wheler is mentioned in 1629. The record is continuous after 1799, when Nymans was inherited by Elizabeth Ellyat. Her son sold it to Thomas Cooper in 1823, Cooper's son George sold it to Thomas Hill in 1837 and in 1839 it was bought by George Harrington. Harrington added more land and probably enlarged and modernised an existing house; it was almost certainly he who planted the newly fashionable evergreen trees which later gave it such an attractive setting. He died before his garden had time to mature, in 1852, and Nymans passed to William Carr. In 1864 the estate was bought by Captain John Dearden, who was to remain in possession for the next twenty-six years.

During the early part of Queen Victoria's reign the industrial revolution had little impact on the southern counties and the population of Sussex remained almost feudal in its ways, relying upon farming and its attendant trades for subsistence. But this age-old economy was gradually forced to change and by 1870 most rural areas of England had entered a long, slow decline. Farmers suffered from the importation of cheap food, profits from wool or corn dwindled, poverty and decay set in. Although the Victorians exulted in their industrial successes and the growth of foreign trade, confidence in the benefits of mechanisation soon faltered. The town-dwelling middle classes, comfortably housed, well fed and educated, began to develop a deep nostalgia for rural life – vague, medieval, romantic – and for its imagined virtues. Country poverty seemed merely picturesque; cottages wreathed in flowers and fields of golden corn were potent symbols of the old Arcadia. Writers and artists ministered to the mood; the message was plain: urban man must go back to his roots and find spiritual refreshment in the country.

The most beautiful and easily accessible counties for Londoners were those which lay directly to the south. The railways had made travel easy, land was cheap, a cottage (or better still, a large house with every modern convenience) became eminently desirable. By the 1880s the rush to the country was in full spate; the Kentish orchards, the Surrey heathlands and the hilly Sussex Weald were so popular with City men that these areas were soon dubbed 'the stockbroker belt'. When Nymans, a medium-sized agricultural estate with a good family house at its centre came on the market in 1890 its purchaser, predictably, was a successful stockbroker.

To country folk someone from the next village could be classed as a stranger, so the new owner of Nymans must have come as something of a shock to the inhabitants of Handcross. Ludwig Messel, a towns-man all his life, short and very dark, speaking English with a strong German accent, was strange in every way. Gossip and speculation would have run wild in the local shops and taverns when the news broke. Yet this foreigner and his descendants were to do more to make Nymans famous than any of its previous English owners.

Ludwig Messel's antecedents were Jewish. The first member of the family about whom anything is known is his grandfather, Aron, born in 1784. During the late eighteenth and early nineteenth century laws were passed in different parts of Europe ordering all Jews to have surnames: it is not clear if Aron or his parents were the first to choose to be called after their home town of Messel. This was a few miles outside Darmstadt, the capital of the Duchy of Hesse, one of the many small states into which Germany was divided at the time. In 1816 Aron Messel founded a banking house in Darmstadt which prospered so well that he soon became a man of considerable wealth and local import-ance. He trained up his eldest son to take over the business and allowed his artistically gifted second son, Simon, to study in Paris. But the eldest son was lost on a journey to America and on Aron's death in 1846 Simon felt obliged to abandon his promising career as a maker of high quality marquetry furniture. He returned to Darmstadt to run the bank and that same year married Emilie Lindheim. Her father was a close

The garden of the Grand Duke's Palace, Bessungen, near Darmstadt

friend and also Chancellor to the hereditary Grand Duke of Hesse, Ludwig III, whose sister had married the Tsar of Russia. Simon Messel adapted well to his new career, assisting the Grand Duke, the Tsar and several other important personages with their financial affairs. The Messel bank went from strength to strength and the family were able to live in style.

Simon and Emilie Messel's first child was born in 1847 and named Ludwig, after the Grand Duke. Four more children followed: Rudolph, Lina, Alfred and Eugenie. In 1859 Simon was travelling abroad and decided to visit the battlefield of Solferino where Alexander of Hesse, the Grand Duke's brother, had recently distinguished himself. Unfortunately Simon contracted typhoid fever here and died after a short illness, aged only forty-two. He left his wife and children well provided for but as his eldest son was only twelve years old the bank was taken over by a relative, Ferdinand Sander. Emilie Messel married again a few years later and her children do not seem to have retained an interest in the family business. However, the boys were given a good education and all three were to be remarkably successful in their chosen careers. Ludwig inherited his father's financial acumen as well as his artistic eye; Rudolph became a scientist and Alfred an architect.

In 1862 the Grand Duke's nephew and heir, Prince Louis of Hesse, married Princess Alice, Queen Victoria's second daughter. This alliance was joyfully greeted by the people of Hesse and Alice devoted herself to the improvement of conditions for the poor and sick in her adopted country. However, she found life in Darmstadt very restricted and dull after England, which both politically and industrially was the most advanced nation in the world. Hesse, a small and backward-looking state, had little to offer its citizens and the brief Austro-Prussian war of 1866, in which the Grand Duke supported the loser, was a financial disaster for the country. Heavy reparations were demanded by Prussia and in the lean times which followed the two elder Messel boys decided to try life abroad.

The date on which Ludwig and Rudolph Messel first arrived in England is not known. Family tradition says they came with gold coins sewn into their shirts; most likely they carried good introductions also. By 1868 – perhaps earlier – Ludwig had a job in London as a clerk in the newly opened branch of an American firm, the stockbrokers Seligman Bros. Rudolph may have returned to Darmstadt to finish his studies as he was not employed in England until 1870, when he became assistant to Sir Henry Roscoe in Manchester, doing chemical research. Ludwig must have settled happily into his new life as he soon invited his seventeen-year-old sister Lina to pay him a visit. He introduced her to the head of his firm, Isaac Seligman, who at once fell in love with her; the couple were married in January 1869. They purchased a property in Lower Tulse Hill which they named Lincoln House, in memory of the assassinated American President, who had been a friend of the Seligman family.

Just over two years later Ludwig himself was married from Lincoln House, so he may have lodged with his employer. His bride, Annie Cussans, was the daughter of an army officer whose forebears had owned sugar plantations in Jamaica. As these had dwindled in value since the abolition of the slave trade, it seems unlikely that Annie, one of eleven children, brought much dowry to her bridegroom. Her parents had both died (within a week of each other) in the spring of 1870.

Ludwig and Annie's marriage took place in Brixton Unitarian Chapel on 19 April 1871. Annie had a Quaker grandmother, which may explain the choice of a Nonconformist chapel, but in later life she attended Church of England services. Little is known about Ludwig's religious views. Although the young Messels had been born into a Jewish family it would appear that all of them, except possibly Lina, had become Christians by the time they reached adulthood. Rudolf

Ludwig and Annie Messel, soon after their marriage in April 1871

never married, but Ludwig, Alfred, and their other sister Eugenie (who also made a life in England) were all married and buried in the Christian faith. If baptised in Hesse, Ludwig would most likely have chosen the Lutheran Church, so a Unitarian chapel in London may have been the most satisfactory compromise when he and Annie decided to marry.

The young Messels made their first home at 34 Wiltshire Road, Brixton. Here two children were born, Leonard in 1872 and Ottilie in 1873. Ludwig soon felt able to leave Seligman Bros and set up a firm of his own: in 1873 the Commercial Directory listed Ludwig Messel, Stock and Share Broker, for the first time. The address was 21 Throgmorton Street, hard by the Stock Exchange and the Bank of England. The firm of L. Messel prospered exceedingly and moved its premises several times: in 1879 it was at 10 Angel Court, in 1894 at 5 Tokenhouse Yard, in 1900 at 66 Old Broad Street. In 1910 the firm returned to Throgmorton Street, this time to No. 31.

By 1874 the Messels were living in Kensington, a newly-fashionable area of town north of the river. They purchased a pleasant detached three-storey stucco-fronted house at 5 Pembridge Villas, and here three more children were brought into the world. In 1878 Ludwig became a naturalised British subject, and by 1880 he was sufficiently wealthy (astute dealings in South African gold were said to be the basis of his fortune) to consider moving house again. This time Ludwig and Annie chose the area – sometimes called Tyburnia – which lay between Hyde Park and Paddington Station. They settled at 8 Westbourne Terrace, where imposing blocks of houses, six storeys high, were set back from the wide main road. Each section of terrace had its own carriage drive with a row of trees and shrubs in front, but there was no garden at the back, just a tiny yard for the servants, overlooked by closely packed houses of a smaller and less prosperous kind. Inside the Messels' house everything was on an impressive scale: big rooms, high ceilings, heavy cornices, endless flights of stairs. This rather ponderous style was attractive to wealthy Germanic immigrants, and Tyburnia, with its good communications, was especially favoured by City men. Here Ludwig had neighbours whose backgrounds were similar to his own: Isidore Spielman at 2 Westbourne Terrace, Arthur Sebag-Montefiore at No. 13, and Edward Lazard at No. 29.

The census of 1881 gives a list of the occupants of each house, their age and status. Ludwig and Annie were both thirty-four that year; their children were Leonard nine, Ottilie eight, Ruth six, Harold four and Hilda two. (Muriel was a late addition to the family, not born until 1889.) Most households in Westbourne Terrace consisted of at least five servants; at No. 8 there were seven, one of whom was a manservant. The cook, Louisa Muckle, was German, but the two nursemaids, two housemaids and a kitchenmaid were English girls.

The Messels filled their new house with beautiful things. The fashion of the day demanded a maximum display of available wealth; furnishings and drapes were heavy and dark, silver massive, ornaments profuse. However, Ludwig was developing a connoisseur's eye; everything had to be the best of its kind, and he seems to have avoided the vulgar trap of excessive ostentation. Twenty-five years after the move to Westbourne Terrace his American daughter-in-law commented on the good taste shown by all the family. She was enormously impressed by the extreme simplicity, combined with the finest materials money could buy, which typified everything in the Messel home.

Ludwig had many interests beside that of making money in the City. He especially loved music and painting, and Victorian London offered ample opportunities to enjoy both. Private music parties were very popular; the English composer Arthur Sullivan and his librettist W.S. Gilbert (known to the children as 'Uncle Schwenck') both became friends and their work was much enjoyed. Artists also flourished; books and periodicals were lavishly illustrated in black and white, and there was a great demand for modern oil paintings. In 1895 Ludwig commissioned a full-length portrait of Annie from Solomon J. Solomon, one of the leading artists of the day. Later, in 1893, he asked Marcus Stone to paint a head-and-shoulders of Ottilie, his eldest daughter.

Some of Ludwig's own quite competent watercolours survive and he made several friends among the artistic community. One such was Linley Sambourne, a cartoonist who worked for the popular and prestigious weekly magazine *Punch*. Sambourne's wife, Marion, was the daughter of Spencer Herapath, a stockbroker with an office almost next door to that of L. Messel in Angel Court. Herapath entertained the Messels at his home in Kensington. Here they met the Sambournes and this contact no doubt led to other introductions: once within the circle it was easy to join the round of private exhibitions and mutual entertainment which the artists enjoyed.

The real importance of the Messel–Sambourne friendship lay in the future union of their children, Leonard and Maud, but in the meantime there was another bonus. Both Marion and Linley Sambourne kept diaries which give a fascinating picture of daily life in middle class London. The colourful social background is evoked by the long lists of parties which the Sambournes attended. Among these the name of

Rowing on the lake. Ludwig Messel with his daughters, Ruth, Hilda and Muriel

Messel crops up at intervals, providing clues to life at 8 Westbourne Terrace. Marion Sambourne and Annie Messel met quite often, either in their own houses or when making rounds of afternoon calls. The Sambournes dined with the Messels a few times and went once to a dance at their house. On another occasion Marion wrote in her diary, 'To Messels, very jolly party, good fun at supper', but most entries make it clear that she felt at a disadvantage, the Messels being so very rich and grand. The little Sambournes, Maud and Roy, went once to a pantomime with the Messel children and were also invited to Westbourne Terrace for big post-Christmas parties, from which they would return laden with toys. On 3 January 1889 Maud, then aged thirteen, attended one of these parties wearing a red dress in which her mother thought she 'looked very sweet'. One wonders if sixteen-year-old Leonard Messel noticed her on that occasion, or if Annie cast an approving eye over this shy, well-behaved little girl. It was a mother's duty to plan ahead, for sons as well as daughters; the Sambournes might not be wealthy but they were stylish, pleasant and, most important, English to the core.

Although the Messel boys were probably sent away to boarding school from the age of eight or so, the girls were educated at home. Hyde Park, only a few minutes' walk from the house, was their playground but even its ample acreage was a poor substitute for a garden. Like most middle class families the Messels escaped from smoky London to the country or the seaside (where holiday lodgings abounded) every year, but by the time a sixth child was born it was time to make more permanent arrangements. Ludwig was not yet in a position to retire from business but he could certainly afford a second home.

In their search for an ideal retreat the Messels naturally looked to see where others of their kind had settled. Whether at that time Ludwig had any aspirations towards the making of a garden is questionable, but his appreciation of beautiful things was never in doubt. The area of the Sussex Weald he chose conformed exactly to the Victorian rural dream, while the situation of the house at Nymans, on a hilltop 450 feet above sea level, was exceptionally fine. There was no view westwards but to the east the land dropped sharply into a narrow, thickly wooded valley before climbing again to a high ridge. Southwards the country rolled more gently; on the horizon, blue and misty, lay the Downs; beyond them, Brighton and the sea. The prospect, so beautiful, so

Nymans, the country home in Sussex which the Messels bought in 1890. Shown here is the south-west front

quintessentially English, has not changed since Ludwig Messel first saw it. A railway viaduct spanned low-lying land in the far distance and one or two rooftops may have shown above the trees, but no other work of man was visible, nor is it today. But just beyond the limit of the view the countryside is cruelly threatened. Haywards Heath to the east and Horsham to the west were, like Crawley, quiet little market towns: now they are sprawling dormitories for London. Gatwick is only a few miles away, Brighton and its satellite towns devour sea-shore and cliff. The London to Brighton road, always a busy thoroughfare, was not quite within sight or hearing of Nymans; today the dual carriageway in its deep cutting generates a ceaseless roar.

The estate the Messels bought was approximately 600 acres in extent. Half of this was agricultural land, with two farmhouses and several cottages for the workers. The garden round the house – called the pleasure grounds in those days – was four acres, perhaps less. Beyond its perimeter fence was some parkland and about two hundred acres of steeply sloping woodland, oak, ash and beech, which provided the shooting so beloved of Victorian landowners. In the valley bottom was a stream and a small lake, possibly a relic of iron-smelting in earlier times. The walled kitchen garden with adjacent head gardener's cottage lay some distance from the house, on the road which linked the villages of Handcross and Staplefield. Staplefield was the more picturesque of the two; it had a cluster of pretty houses, a green on which cricket was played, and the parish church.

With his purchase Ludwig gained a drawing of the house and garden as they had looked some years earlier. This shows a severe but ample Regency or early Victorian villa. Tall south-facing windows look across a large expanse of lawn in which a few round flower beds have been cut; here a crinolined lady with a sunshade is instructing a gardener. Two semi-mature trees (a monkey-puzzle and a Morinda spruce) occupy the foreground. Both these trees have since fallen, but the artist would have been positioned beneath a cedar of Lebanon which still stands and is now the oldest tree in the garden. The main entrance to the house appears to be in the centre of a low wing on the north-west side, under a lean-to glass verandah or conservatory. It is a charming view of a perfect gentleman's residence, such as would bring a gleam to the eye of any house-hunter today.

However, by the standards of 1890 the house was thoroughly old-fashioned and dull. Like all new owners Ludwig and Annie had plenty of ideas for its improvement and an architect was called in at once. His name was Leonard Stokes, brother of the artist Adrian Stokes who was one of the Sambournes' acquaintances. He soon had a sketch scheme ready for his client and this drawing was exhibited in the Royal Academy the following year, entitled 'Nymans, near Crawley, showing additions and alterations for L. Messel, Esq.' For some reason these proposals were either never carried out, or were abandoned half-way through, and another architect, Ernest George, was responsible for the next stage of the work.

Ernest George and his partner, Harold Peto, were experienced house builders who had transformed large areas of South Kensington with terracotta and red brick in a Flemish Renaissance style. They also built several vast and elaborate country houses in the Jacobean taste. Two of these, Buchan Hill (now called Cottesmore House) and Balcombe Park, were very close to Nymans; although no longer private homes they give an excellent idea of what the Messels might have aspired to had they been even richer. Ernest George's drawings for Nymans have not survived but the ground plan (which can still be traced today) was remarkably similar to that shown on Stokes's drawing. From this one can deduce that Ludwig's alterations were largely cosmetic: he was not prepared to go to the expense of a whole new house. The Regency villa and its north-west wing remained, albeit disguised with lavish

Nymans, the south-west front after alterations. The shape of the original house can still be discerned in the centre, with the conservatory on the left

trimmings and black-and-white work. The chief additions were on the south side – a huge square conservatory at one end, a large billiard room with curious low-slung roof at the other, while an imposing Italianate tower with an open viewing gallery, topped by a miniature cupola, dominated the centre. Over the years more alterations took place: the half-timbering was painted white, the viewing gallery enclosed, a bay window in Regency style and a porch with classical columns added. All these strangely disparate forms were veiled in climbing plants – wisteria, *Clematis montana, Rosa banksiae,* – and wall shrubs. Ludwig and Annie were no doubt delighted with their Victorian fantasy but posterity cannot sit in judgement on their taste: after only thirty years of life, this building made way for yet another dream house.

The employment offered by the new owner of Nymans would have been welcomed in this poor rural community. The house alterations gave work over several years to a team of local labourers and craftsmen; jobs were assured for woodsmen and gamekeepers, gardeners and stablehands, as well as for housemaids, cooks and nurserymaids. Annie Messel was quick to involve herself and her daughters in charity work, and the family's attendance at church forged links with neighbours. Ludwig's leisure time was spent in taking stock of his new acquisition, adding to his house, walking and shooting in the woods, taking tea on the lawn, exulting in possession.

For most Englishmen the purchase of a piece of land marks a high point in their lives – a romantic yearning satisfied, an ambition fulfilled. For the Messels it was all this, and more. Ludwig had renounced the country of his origin to carve a career in England; his sons were English born and bred, and from the first he had made sure that no advantage was denied them. In 1890 Leonard was eighteen, about to leave Eton and go to Oxford; Harold, thirteen, would follow in his brother's footsteps. Ottilie was seventeen, Ruth sixteen and Hilda eleven. Muriel, the little afterthought, was just a year old and thus the only one of the six unable to remember life before Nymans. The children were all devoted to their new home, the ultimate proof that the family were not foreigners, here today and gone tomorrow, but had put down roots. Photographs in a family album show them enjoying every aspect of country life, playing on the lawn, rowing on the lake, and entertaining friends.

No visitors' book exists for these early years but there were always busy comings and goings at Nymans and some of the guests can be traced. In July 1893 the seventeen-year-old Maud Sambourne was invited to spend a fortnight there, ostensibly as a companion for Ruth. The girls had been friendly as children, not only in London but also at Margate, where they had played together on seaside holidays. They were now at an exciting turning point in their lives, just finishing with the schoolroom and poised to enter adult social life.

Maud was artistically gifted and very good-looking – not dark, like the Messel girls but fair skinned with grey-blue eyes. She had been brought up in a close-knit, loving family and although the Sambournes were not poor they were less affluent than most of their friends and relations. Watching her mother's struggle to make each penny do the work of two had made a deep impression and Maud was enormously impressed by everything she saw at Nymans. There were luxuries of every kind, yet the large cheerful family remained simple and kindly, doing their utmost to dispel her shyness and make her stay a happy one. The youngest child, Muriel, made a delightful plaything, and each day was a whirl of activity. Maud wrote regularly to her mother, and from these letters can be gained glimpses of life with the Messels in their country home.

> The house which is a very charming one is situated on the top of a mountain, the view all round is much too magnificent to describe . . . Ruth is watering the plants and does all the little duties of a second daughter. She is a darling, so unselfish and sweet. The German which goes on all round is awfully amusing . . . Baby is playing on the lawn in front with her various sweethearts, she is the most intelligent of children, it seems incredible at the age of only four.

During Maud's stay Leonard returned home from Oxford and Harold from Eton. From the tone of her letters it does not seem as if either of the boys was well-known to her and Lennie she observed carefully. He was twenty-one, short and dark like his father, but good-looking, affectionate and merry.

> It is quite sweet to see Mr Lennie with his mother, the devotion one rarely sees in a boy. He won't allow her to do a thing and when she looks worried he sits by her all the time and strokes her hand . . . It does one quite good to be with Ruth she is so good and dear to everyone and has the most tremendous influence over her brothers. They simply adore her and baby also. Mr Lennie is very kind to me and so are they all. Ruth said she would have to get quite jealous

Leonard Messel, at Oxford when he was an undergraduate at Merton College, 1893

because Mrs Messel never likes any girls but her own. I don't think I ever stayed in such a jolly house and only wish you were here to enjoy the lovely country as I do . . .

Like the rest of the family Lennie was great fun and very soon Maud had dropped the 'Mr'. They laughed and joked together and he helped her to make dolls for Ruth's Sunday School children. Maud, for all her innocence, was already aware of the strange effect her presence often wrought on the opposite sex and Lennie showed every sign of being smitten, although he was too uncertain of his future that summer to do any serious courting.

Unknown to the Messel parents, another romance had already begun. Lennie made several good friends at Merton College, Oxford, among them two scholars, Max Beerbohm and Eric Parker. Eric had very little money (his mother had to bring up several children, of whom Eric was the eldest, singlehanded) and Lennie invited him several times to Nymans. The kindly welcome and luxurious surroundings there were much appreciated, and these visits led to his first paid employment. Young Harold was being prepared for entry into

Eton, so it was arranged for Eric to give him some extra tutoring during the school holidays. But something not envisaged was that Eric might fall in love with Ruth, and she with him. Both were very young when they first met (he was twenty, she sixteen) but were at once convinced that they were made for each other. Naturally when Ludwig discovered this affair he was not pleased; Eric he thought was too much of a poet, and too impractical ever to make his way in the world. He sent the young man packing (allowed to return only if he could prove earnings of £2,000 a year) and Ruth had to nurse her love affair in secret for many years. If this suffering was ever confided to her friends, no hint of it was passed on in Maud's letters home.

Davidia involucrata

Chapter Two

Planting Begins

T he house at Nymans which Maud decribed as 'very charming' was not the final version, although it is difficult to tell how much alteration had been carried out by the time of her visit. Certainly its surroundings were not much changed by then from those shown in the little drawing which Ludwig had bought with the property, and no evidence survives to indicate whether he knew, or cared, anything about gardening. However, the Messels would certainly have hoped to be integrated with the local gentry and it cannot have been long before they realised that many of their more desirable neighbours were interested not just in shooting, the favourite sport of so many wealthy Victorians, but in all forms of animal and plant life. Several of them were naturalists of great repute and as landowners were able to investigate one particular aspect of their vocation in depth: they were passionate and innovative gardeners.

One property which shared a boundary with Nymans was The High Beeches, home of Wilfred Loder. His father, Robert Loder, descendant of a long line of west-country yeomen, had bought land here in 1849; he greatly enlarged an existing house and laid out extensive formal gardens in the manner of the time. Created baronet in 1887, sometime Member of Parliament for Shoreham and High Sheriff of Sussex, Robert Loder had a distinguished career. He raised a family of seven sons at The High Beeches, and the name of Loder was to become well known in the horticultural world, even to the third and fourth generation. It was Sir Robert's eldest son, Edmund, who made the family's first, and possibly greatest, contribution to the art of gardening.

In 1878 Edmund Loder married the daughter of William Hubbard of Leonardslee. This estate, near Horsham on the edge of the ancient St Leonard's Forest, lay a few miles to the west of both The High Beeches and Nymans and was in many ways similar to them. In each case an old house on high ground commanded splendid southerly views across a thickly wooded valley. The Hubbards had lived at Leonardslee since

1852 and although they had enlarged the house the estate remained much as they found it, mostly parkland well stocked with native trees. North of the house some cedars, redwoods, magnolias and rhododendrons had been grouped, probably in the 1830s, in what was then termed an 'American Garden'. In 1888 Edmund Loder succeeded to his father's title and the following year acquired Leonardslee from his parents-in-law, leaving The High Beeches to be taken over by his brother next in age, Wilfred.

Sir Edmund Loder was gifted in many spheres. Much travelled, an expert botanist, astronomer and photographer, he was also a crack rifle shot and famed big-game hunter. He at once began to make a wild-life park at Leonardslee with wallabies, emus, beavers, Sika deer and other rare animals roaming freely in large paddocks. He also extended the garden with several ambitious schemes. A large number of coniferous trees were added to those already planted, so that within a few years the pinetum at Leonardslee included almost every cone-bearing tree known to science. Alpines were well represented and a splendid rockery was designed and built by the foremost experts of the day, Messrs Pulham and Sons. Daffodils were another speciality, while in a sheltered corner of the grounds palms, bamboos and citrus trees made an impressive 'sub-tropical walk'. Sir Edmund was particularly interested in correct nomenclature and taxonomy, and any new introductions from foreign lands, especially flowering trees and shrubs, were eagerly collected. Much trial and error was needed to discover which of the exotics could flourish unprotected in the English climate. Camellias, for instance, were for a long time considered tender; some were planted near the house, where they grew huge and astonished the horticultural world by surviving frosts which cut laurel to the ground.

There was everything a keen gardener could desire at Leonardslee – an orchid house and a rose garden (the special preserve of Lady Loder) among other delights – but Sir Edmund, who could have constructed stepped terraces with statuary in the Italian manner on his steeply-sloping site, had little enthusiasm for the grand or formal style of gardening. Instead, the land below the house was developed as a woodland garden. Rough paths wound down into the valley where a series of ponds were enlarged into a chain of small lakes. On the lakeshore, and in clearings between the trees, thousands of rhododendrons, azaleas and other flowering shrubs were planted in irregular groups or drifts to look as if they were growing naturally. The result was a more dramatic, colourful and varied landscape than had ever been seen in England before.

Just across the road from Leonardslee was another big house, South Lodge, built by the distinguished naturalist Frederick Godman. In 1861 Godman had made the first of several expeditions to Guatemala, collecting information on the flora and fauna of the area; a few years later he began to edit what was to be a work of the first importance, *Biologia Centrali Americana*. This eventually ran to sixty-three quarto volumes with over 1,600 plates, describing 19,000 species new to science. From 1883 onwards Godman's spare time was spent in the creation of a fine garden at South Lodge, where he mingled rare plants with English natives to fine effect. He and Sir Edmund became good friends.

Any horticulturist at that time would have been familiar with the ideas of William Robinson, one of the most influential gardening writers of the century. Born in Ireland in 1838, Robinson began life as a garden boy and was largely self-educated. In 1861 he went to work at the Royal Botanic Society's garden in Regent's Park, London, and from there toured other botanic gardens up and down the country, making notes and collecting unusual plants. He started writing articles for the *Gardeners' Chronicle* in 1863, and in 1871 launched his own horticultural journal, *The Garden*. Throughout his long life (he died aged ninety-seven in 1935) he begged gardeners to follow nature's lead, not impose stiff patterns on the landscape. He especially abhorred the 'bedding-out' so very popular at the time, and never lost an opportunity to denigrate any scheme he saw in which flowers were heartlessly regimented into blocks or rows of strident colour. All his writing emphasised the beauty of individual plants and the pleasures to be derived from wild flowers in meadows and hedgerows, or from hardy plants and shrubs growing free and unconstrained. His book *The English Flower Garden*, published in 1883, is his best known work but before that he had written on alpine plants, hardy plants and what he called the 'Wild Garden'. His forthright articles made him many enemies, but his tireless campaigning did in the end alter public taste, although Robinson's name is less revered today than that of his disciple, Gertrude Jekyll.

By 1885 Robinson had made enough money from his writings to buy himself a retirement home at Gravetye in Sussex, about ten miles east of Leonardslee and South Lodge, where he could lay out a new garden and plant up a big estate on the principles he had preached for so long. His house was ancient and picturesque but the garden round it had the usual mid-century Wellingtonias and spruces which Robinson cut down, planting instead quantities of native trees – 120,000 by 1890 –

Plate 1   *Prunus subhirtilla rosea* and dafffodils in the Wall Garden

Plate 2 Nymans. The west front and dovecote

Plate 3 Wakehurst Place. The Himalayan Glade

Plate 4 Sheffield Park. mView across the lake

Plate 5 The High Beeches. Bluebells and rhododendrons in the spring

Plate 6   Leonardslee. Azaleas in the valley

Plate 7   Nymans. The copper
beech and yew hedge

Plate 8a   Rhododendron prinophyllum 'Philip Holmes'

Plate 8b   Rhododendron 'Thomas Messel'

Plate 8c   Rhododendron cerasinum 'Herbert Mitchell'

Plate 8d   Rhododendron 'Leonard Messel'

Paintings by Victoria Messel

Plate 9   Rhododendrons by the tennis lawn

mixed with hardy flowering shrubs. A lake was created, daffodils were naturalised in the meadows, with primroses, bluebells and other wild flowers encouraged to seed everywhere.

Although William Robinson was now a landowner, it would have taken some time before he was welcomed socially by the Loders and other well-placed local families, even though they were pleased to show him round their gardens and ask his advice. Barriers between the classes at that time were hard to surmount; at Nymans, Ludwig Messel with his City connections may have found it just as difficult to enter the world of the Sussex squirarchy as the garden boy from Ireland. Ludwig was disadvantaged in other ways too: neither a scientist nor a sportsman, with no traveller's tales to tell, he had little in common with those he might wish to make his friends. At Nymans the pleasure grounds were sadly undeveloped and that essential adjunct of a gentleman's residence, a conservatory full of the newest and most expensive plants imported from sub-tropical lands, was lacking. But these defects could be remedied: Ludwig had the money to make a fine showing; only the will had, so far, been absent. If he expressed an interest in gardening and requested help from his knowledgeable and enthusiastic neighbours, the entrée to a new world of pleasure might be his.

The exact point at which Ludwig felt bold enough to ask advice is not known, but he was always conscious how much he, and his garden, owed to the encouragement given by both Sir Edmund Loder and William Robinson. The first indication of gardening fever at Nymans came early in 1895, when plans for a large new conservatory on the south-west corner of the house were put in hand. But before the new building was completed the Messels' head gardener had departed. Possibly he was too old and set in his ways to undertake the schemes which may already have been taking shape in Ludwig's mind. No visitor to Leonardslee or Gravetye could have failed to be impressed by the originality of the planting there: someone energetic and forward-looking would have to be found if the Messels were to create anything comparable. A young man called James Comber was recommended for the post and it was his appointment in September 1895 that marked the real beginning of the garden at Nymans.

James Comber [pronounced 'Coomber'] was born in 1866 on a small farm in Ashdown Forest, not far from Nymans. The family had lived off the land in this part of Sussex for generations and could trace their line back to 1600. James was one of eight children, a clever boy, keen on music and books, eager and willing to learn. He liked to help his father in the garden, digging and weeding, and was nine years old when he sent off his first seed order to Messrs Suttons. In those days there was little chance of higher education for a farmer's son, but there were several trades which offered an ambitious hard-working lad a way to the top. One of these was gardening. Even the smallest country estate employed a staff of several gardeners, and to be Head Gardener for a wealthy or aristocratic landowner was a job which carried considerable prestige.

The nearest big estate to the Combers' home was Wakehurst Place, then owned by the Dowager Marchioness of Downshire. Wakehurst had belonged to the Culpeper family from 1468 to 1694 and the fine Elizabethan mansion was still standing. In 1879 young Comber began his career here, walking the two miles between his home and Wakehurst Place every morning and evening. As garden boy he was paid 5s. a week for a working day which began at 6 a.m. and lasted until 5.30 p.m., but in spite of the long hours he still found time at home to raise collections of verbena and hardy ferns which won first prizes at Cuckfield Show in 1880 and 1881. After three years, on the recommendation of Joseph Cheal (founder of Lowfield Nurseries at Crawley) Comber moved to Dencombe, a property on the road between Nymans and The High Beeches, where he held the post of 'improver' at 12s. a week; this sum had to cover food and lodgings as well as 1s. premium to the head gardener. The lack of books here was the severest privation, but by careful saving he was able to buy Thomson's *Gardener's Assistant*; he also borrowed Loudon's *Encyclopaedia* from his grandfather, and studied assiduously in his spare time. Three years at Dencombe were followed by another three years as 'journeyman' at Tilgate, a large garden (again close to Nymans) owned by John Nix.

In the spring of 1888 Comber moved to the nursery of Messrs J. Veitch and Sons at Coombe Wood, near Kingston upon Thames. This famous firm, founded in 1808 and originally established in Devon, specialised in rare plants. Many of these were brought back by their own collectors from South America, California and the Far East so that the greenhouses were full of exciting things. Although the new recruit earned a reprimand for lingering to take notes, he also formed a lasting friendship with John Heal, Veitch's expert raiser and exhibitor of rarities. The placing of gardeners was another of the firm's enterprises and they soon sent Comber to Ashby St Ledgers Lodge, Rugby, where after a few months he was promoted to foreman. About this time he began writing articles for magazines, among them Robinson's publication, *The Garden*.

In search of more experience and higher wages, Comber went on to Drinkstone Park, near Bury St Edmunds in Suffolk. The countryside round about was very different from Sussex and he enjoyed collecting wild flowers as well as visiting all the good gardens in the district. He also met Ethel Lambert, a pupil-teacher about to go to Norwich Training College. She studied botany and lent him notes and textbooks which he read eagerly. In 1892 Comber's employer died and after a brief spell at Longford Castle, Salisbury, he was offered the post of Head Gardener at Bignor Park, near Petworth in Sussex. Two years later, aged twenty-nine, experienced in all branches of horticulture and with excellent recommendations, he came to work for Ludwig Messel.

James Comber took up his position as Head Gardener at Nymans on 11 September 1895. What made him its devoted servant for the rest of his long life? Until he went there he had been always on the move, avid for new experience, keen to prove himself. But the time had come to settle down, perhaps marry. The cottage that went with the job was a good one, commanding as fine a southerly view as the big house: Ethel Lambert might be willing to share it with him. Although the estate was

James Comber, in 1892

a fair size, the garden was not large and the staff employed probably fewer in number than Comber had had under him at Bignor Park. But the wages Ludwig Messel offered were apparently much better – an important consideration at a time when the agricultural depression was severely affecting all those who worked on the land. (Indoor servants up at the house earned far more than the gardeners and estate workers.) Comber knew this corner of Sussex very well; he might have been friendly with the previous gardener at Nymans and would have realised that the soil, loam over sandstone, was remarkably fertile and easy to work, while frost drained quickly away down the slopes. Plants grew and flourished here in a way which made visiting gardeners, both then and now, feel green with envy.

Quite likely Ludwig Messel made it clear that he had money to spend and held out promises of expansion and improvements. One would like to think also that the two men summed each other up favourably from their first meeting, although they could not have been more different in background and education. Even physically they looked incongruous together: Comber, tall and thin, kept his fine figure to the end of his days, towering above every member of the family he was to serve so well for fifty-eight years.

It is always difficult, when a partnership is outstandingly successful, to apportion praise. Ludwig Messel was a man of energy and vision at the peak of a successful career. He was also an experienced collector of things rare and beautiful and had an artist's eye of great refinement. At Nymans Comber supplied the basic horticultural expertise, without which the new venture would have foundered, but something else equally important – a sympathy with his employer's aims and ideals. Head gardeners could be an intractable breed; many Victorian owners deplored the obstinacy of faithful servants who continued to do things their own way whatever the master said. Comber ruled in the kitchen-garden, the glasshouses and the flower borders, deploying his staff to keep all spick and span, mow the lawns and rake the drive, but it was undoubtedly Ludwig's enthusiasm which led to so much experiment in other departments. Each sparked off the other with new ideas, suggestions, plans. Ludwig had found not just a gardener, but someone to share in the great creative adventure of his latter years. Comber had found his life's work.

During the winter of 1895/6 Comber had time to take stock and plan improvements. The new conservatory was the first project to need attention and it was soon planted up with extravagant and exciting purchases: banana trees and *Strelitzia reginae* would both grow roof-high in time, *Araucaria excelsa* nearly as large. Colourful climbers, white and red lapageria, *Tecoma grandiflora* and *Streptosolen jamesonii* wreathed the columns, with pots of geraniums banked along the shelves. Warmed by hot water pipes in winter, shaded by long blinds in summer, the conservatory would have had a more equable climate than the rest of the house and was a favourite place for the family to gather.

High on the list of things for Comber to do was a complete overhaul of the kitchen garden. A head gardener's chief task was to organise a constant supply of fresh fruit and vegetables for the mansion, enough not only for the family when they were in residence but for their town house during the London season. Each morning a basket of produce would be delivered to Cook, and woe betide the gardener if she was not satisfied with his offerings. Any sudden influx of visitors had to be catered for also, with fruit from the hothouse – melons, grapes and pineapples, even out-of-season strawberries – essential ingredients for a successful dinner party. A wide choice of indoor plants and fresh flowers was important too; only in exceptional circumstances would the mistress be expected to arrange a vase of flowers in the drawing room or place a bowl of fruit on the dining table. Such jobs were the responsibility of the head gardener, and jealously guarded. Although there is no record of the number of staff employed at Nymans in the 1890s, by the outbreak of the First World War (when the garden had been considerably enlarged) Comber had ten men under him – five for the kichen garden and five for the pleasure grounds.

In 1895 the garden proper probably consisted of little more than the large expanse of lawn surrounded by banks of azaleas and tall *Rhododendron arboreum*, which provided plenty of colour in May. (These rhododendrons layer easily, and their progeny can still be seen today.) Several photographs taken of the house about this time show the high standard of gardening achieved in the days when labour was no problem: the carefully trained creepers on the façade, the well-planted tubs and sculpted topiary along the south front, the rose beds and the plump evergreens beside the immaculate sweep of gravel drive which led up to the front door. Another photograph shows the gardener's cottage looking just as neat and prosperous, its porch hung with roses and clematis, the central path edged with box and the narrow borders on either side packed with plants. James Comber and Ethel Lambert were married in August 1898; this flower-decked cottage was home to them for the rest of their lives.

While Comber worked hard to get the existing garden up to standard, Ludwig had plenty of time to stroll around his domain deciding on new effects. His first desire was for a Pinetum. This, like a conservatory, was the preserve of every gentleman: big cone-bearing trees, especially those from North America, had been highly valued for over a century. There were good examples of such planting on several estates nearby; besides Wakehurst Place and Leonardslee there was Warnham Court, near Horsham, owned by the Lucas family who became friends of the Messels. The firm of Veitch (especially well known for their conifers) had been employed in 1880 to set out the Pinetum there. As Comber had worked for Veitch, it is likely that their nurseries would have been approached to supply young plants for Nymans also.

A sloping, open site some distance to the north of the house was chosen for the Pinetum, and plans were drawn up for planting in a wide horseshoe curve. The trees were not planted in botanical orders but carefully selected for their variety of form and colour. Old favourites were mingled with newly introduced species; those which would in time grow very large were interplanted with shorter, stouter specimens. Great skill is needed to make satisfactory groupings as so many variables have to be taken into account. To protect the young trees a belt of quick-growing spruce was provided; eventually all would knit together to create a fine wind-break, sheltering the rest of the garden from the fierce north-easterly gales. The first trees were in the ground before the end of 1896; more were planted in 1898 and additions continued to be made for several years. From the highest point of the field, in the centre of the curve, a marvellous view extended across Balcombe Forest to Crowborough Beacon. Later a summerhouse in the form of a miniature Greek temple was erected here, to a design by Ludwig's architect brother Alfred. Alfred Messel was also responsible for another feature, a viewing platform jutting out over the valley near the east side of the house, known as 'The Prospect'.

The Pinetum was only the first phase in Ludwig's plans for his garden; new ideas, new plantings, proceeded apace. In 1902 an arboretum was begun, extending from the Pinetum eastwards down the hill, but most of the early developments were on the south side of the house, beyond the lawn. A ha-ha separated the pleasure ground from the park and along this boundary several important features were created. First a croquet lawn was cut out of the slope and the resulting steep escarpments were made into a rock wall and a rock garden, again popular features of the time. The rock garden was much smaller than the huge affair at Leonardslee, although the same contractors, Messrs Pulham and Sons, were called in. Real sandstone, not the artificial

The new Heath Garden, looking north *c.* 1902

rockwork which was the Pulham speciality, was used and a fine range of aubretias, helianthemums and arenarias, mixed with dwarf shrubs such as cistus, cotoneaster and veronica, were planted here.

More original use was made of the piece of uneven ground just east of the croquet lawn. Here Ludwig made a Heath Garden, possibly the first of its kind to be seen in England. Although ericas were sometimes planted in the wilder parts of gardens, Nymans seems to have been the earliest to have a special area devoted to these plants. Ludwig had seen a few growing together near King William's Temple at Kew and had thought at once that they would be ideally suited to the sandy loam at Nymans. He and Comber mulled over the idea together and decided to shape the ground into hillocks, divided by small winding paths. Ericas, callunas and their allies – about fifty varieties altogether – were mixed with dwarf rhododendrons, andromedas (*pieris*) and *Rosa microphylla*. *Pinus montana* was added to protect the taller heathers from wind and snow. The result was a great success and in September 1902 the Messels held a garden party for friends and neighbours, no doubt with the express intention of showing off this feature. The idea of a heath garden was soon copied, and in recent years this type of planting has become all too common. The ericas at Nymans have outgrown their allotted space and it is hard now to realise how exciting this part of the pleasure grounds must have seemed in those early days.

Later, more improvements were made here. The Japanese Exhibition held in London in 1903 had a great influence on public taste, both in the home and in gardens. Ludwig obtained some stone lanterns when the exhibition closed and set these among the heaths; he also planted a weeping elm on a mound and surrounded it with ornamental railings in the Japanese manner. To complete the fashionable effect a stretch of pergola was built along the western boundary of the croquet lawn: stone columns supported wooden beams on which *Wisteria sinensis* and *W. multijuga* could show their long racemes to best advantage. As these were slow-growing a number of other climbers were planted for quick effect: actinidia, clematis, honeysuckle and roses.

Other changes were taking place just north of the house, where there was a large paddock (or possibly an old orchard) which could be put to better use. It may already have been partially enclosed with walls and hedges; these were completed to form a sheltered area about one hundred yards across. The layout at first was simple: wide straight paths met at right angles in the centre, the crossing marked with a sundial and four yews. The paths were bordered with flowers but the main planting was of fruit trees. Five varieties of cooking apple and seven of eating apple grew here, including 'Cox's Orange Pippin', 'Beauty of Bath', 'Blenheim Orange' and Ludwig's own favourite, 'Sussex Forge'.

On the western edge of the pleasure grounds, linking the lower part of the Pinetum with the house, a long curving avenue of limes was planted. From here the view across the valley was kept open and wild flowers were encouraged in the meadow, Robinson-style. Paths ran down through the native woods towards the lake in the valley bottom. Here the family went swimming or fishing, had picnics in the summer and skating parties in the winter. Great sheets of bluebells grew in the clearings; rhododendrons and other shrubs were planted here too, in the manner of Leonardslee. But the walk to the lake is a long one and the gradient too steep for someone getting on in years, so this part of the garden was gradually left to its own devices. In contrast, the rich soil and rapidly thickening shelter belts on top of the hill gave Ludwig and his gardener the chance to grow not only rhododendrons but many other exciting new flowering plants nearer the house.

Chapter Three

The Garden Takes Shape

While Ludwig was absorbed in planning his new garden, the Messel children were growing up. Ottilie was the first to become engaged and was married to Ernest Loring, a naval officer, in April 1897. At the same time Lennie was courting Maud Sambourne. He had seen her occasionally since 1893 but much of his time had been spent abroad, working at a bank in Germany. On returning to London in February 1897 he found Maud the centre of an admiring court. No longer an unsophisticated child, she had blossomed into a fascinating beauty, and Lennie proposed to her at once.

Maud was in no mood to accept. For the past three years she had enjoyed a delightful round of visits, parties and balls; she had refused several offers of marriage and was in danger of having her head turned with so much attention. This latest suitor was rejected out of hand: she did not love him, and marriage was out of the question.

Lennie had made up his mind and difficulties only increased his ardour. He made a formal call on Maud's father to ask for her hand but both Linley and Marion Sambourne were firm in their rejection: their daughter had made it plain that she did not wish to marry anyone just yet, and young Leonard Messel 'for many reasons' would not do. One can only guess what these reasons were: although the Sambournes had several friends with German–Jewish backgrounds, marriage into such a family was not to be undertaken lightly. Queen Victoria's German relatives and the Prince of Wales's wealthy Jewish friends were unpopular with a large section of the population, and Lennie, like his father, suffered snubs and affronts all his life from a society which took no trouble to conceal its anti-Semitic bias.

The Messel family all supported Lennie in his choice. Ruth, heartsore at the difficulties her own romance was suffering, begged Maud to make her brother happy, but she showed no sign of softening. Lennie was only able to see his beloved at parties where she ignored him while flirting outrageously with other swains. But by the beginning of July his persistence brought reward and Maud agreed to consider (although not accept) his offer of marriage. Her parents were still against the idea and stipulated that no firm decision should be made until the autumn: Maud was to spend a fortnight with the Messel family at Nymans and then have six weeks with friends in Scotland before giving her final answer.

Maud wrote regularly to her mother from Scotland. She had no wish to give up her freedom and the thought of marriage depressed her. She liked Lennie well enough: he was fun to be with, madly in love, and his prospects were excellent. He would give her everything she wanted, but could she love him? Poor Lennie just had to wait, without even the comfort of a letter, while she struggled to make up her mind. When her holiday was extended, first by one week, then another, his patience cracked and he wrote stiffly to her parents demanding an explanation.

Maud returned to London on 18 October. The next day, still hesitant and rather tearful, she accepted Lennie's offer and became formally engaged. The Messels seem to have been delighted by the news, welcoming her most kindly into the family. The Sambournes were all asked to spend Christmas at Nymans and Marion's diary describes how much she enjoyed the visit. Another couple, friends of the Messels, were guests also; the chief entertainment seems to have been long walks in the woods each day for the ladies and rabbit shooting for the men. The London fog had been very bad that winter so the clear frosty air at Nymans and the beautiful countryside were greatly appreciated. There were lavish Christmas gifts for everyone, and the Sambournes were particularly struck by the number of presents given to the servants.

Once committed, Maud grew happier. She and Lennie paid calls on all their relatives, including the Seligmans, who were now living in great state at 17 Kensington Palace Gardens. The young couple went house-hunting and chose 37 Gloucester Terrace, just round the corner from the Messels' house in Westbourne Terrace, as their first home. Ludwig liked to have his grown-up children living near him: as each in turn married, he gave a substantial sum of money with which to purchase or build a house, the only proviso being that it should be close enough for them to visit him and Annie frequently.

Maud and Lennie were married on 28 April 1898. The union was to prove long and very happy; Lennie's devotion never wavered, and Maud made an ideal wife. Their first child, a boy, was born in London on 31 August 1899, and was christened Linley, after Maud's father. When he was a few weeks old she took him down to stay at Nymans for a time. A letter to her mother shows that Maud rather resented the possessive attitude of her in-laws towards the baby. 'Everyone here looks on him as the future owner of Nymans when all the time he is *quite quite* mine,' she wrote, 'I only hope he will turn out a fair haired blue-eyed youth with a loyal feeling to his mother's side of the family. If he dares to have dark hair, well – I shall dye it golden!'

On 8 February 1902 Maud and Lennie had a second child (named Anne after her paternal grandmother) who was destined to be far more important in the story of Nymans than her elder brother. Lennie was by this time well established in his father's firm and felt the need for his own country estate. His young family had spent previous summers at a house on the Surrey/Sussex borders, but an outbreak of typhoid among the local inhabitants had made Maud nervous. A larger house, standing in its own grounds, was found at Balcombe in Sussex. This had the advantage of being very close to Nymans and Ludwig was happy to advance £8,500 for its purchase. Lennie and Maud moved here in the summer of 1902, but still kept their town house fully staffed for use during part of the year.

Gentle, dutiful Ruth had to wait far longer than Maud for her wedding-day. Eric Parker had set to work to make a career as a journalist, writing articles on nature and sport. When he was appointed Editor of *The Country Gentleman* Ludwig relented at last, and Ruth and Eric were allowed to marry in June 1902. Ludwig did not become entirely reconciled to the match for several years but when he finally admitted that Eric was a worthy son-in-law he gave the young couple enough money to build their own country house. They chose a site near Godalming in Surrey, with a wonderful view, and asked Ernest Newton to be their architect. The house, which they called Feathercombe, was finished in 1911 and Eric made a fine garden here, taking advice from his father-in-law and from Comber, and using many of the plants that had succeeded so well at Nymans.

A year after Ruth's wedding her younger sister, Hilda, was married to Arthur Gibbes and in December 1903 the Messels' second son, Harold, brought home an American bride. He had fallen in love with Leonora Gibson a few years earlier when visiting Hilda at her finishing school in Germany: Leonora was studying music there with the expectation of becoming a concert pianist. Ludwig and Annie had not been best pleased when Harold informed them that he wished to marry; they insisted that he must wait until he was properly established in the family firm. Harold eventually had his way and was married in New York, returning to London after a brief honeymoon. His bride was naturally nervous of meeting her new in-laws but everything went off well. In a series of letters to her mother Leonora left the best description of the Messels' home life that has come down to us:

> 86 Oxford Terrace, 14.12.03. My darling Mama . . . Isn't it an exciting situation, a home of our own, a new country and a new 'family-in-law'. The latter is of course the most difficult to describe on paper . . . They brought us here from the station, tea was ready and they had decorated the rooms most charmingly with palms and flowers. I liked them all from the start and there was nothing strained or awkward. Hilda is charming, very pretty, exquisitely dressed with perfect manners . . . Harold's mother is a very dear old lady with a sense of humour. They none of them speak above a whisper and laugh like a faint little ripple. We were asked to dinner directly and 'Mama-in-law' sent over her maid to unpack for me which she did beautifully, stowing everything away in tissue paper to guard against the fog. I wore my blue and ruby over to dinner as it was *en famille*. As yet I had not encountered his Imperial Majesty, you must remember. But he was on the staircase when we entered and Harold brought me forward solemnly. After saying 'how do you do' conversation flagged when the old man remarked 'I suppose we ought to kiss' but made no move. I forthwith up and kissed him with no more ado. Harold had been called to the telephone and missed the choice scene but he declares that he would willingly have given £5 to have been a witness . . .

(Ludwig and Annie had two grandchildren so Leonora, at nineteen, may be forgiven for thinking them rather old; they were both only fifty-seven). The letter goes on:

> The old gentleman conducted me in state to the drawing room where 'Ma' was standing in magnificent evening dress, very quiet though, black with lots of handsome lace and exquisite pearls and diamonds. A footman announced dinner and we trooped down. A butler with the aid of a second butler served us the meagre repast of nine courses, conversation flourished and I had quite a heart-to-heart with 'Pa'. I like him best of all. Under several layers of his formality there is a genuine personality . . . . The house is beautiful, stately, dignified and innately elegant. Culture wherever you turn, beautiful pictures

which I have not half seen yet. Hilda is simply sweet, she loves all the luxuries but there is not a grain of worldliness about herself, to me most touching. She took me to her dressmaker and shopping yesterday morning and 'Ma' drove us in state in the afternoon in the carriage, showed me Buckingham Palace and the sights . . . . They will insist on our having all our meals at Westbourne Terrace, there seems no way out of it. I was taken back to tea which was handed round by two butlers – it being too hard for one.

A week of parties, theatres and introductions followed – 'Such a rush . . . a storm of new impressions.' It was too much for Harold, who went to bed with neuralgia, and even the buoyant Leonora confessed to feeling rather done-up. Just before Christmas the whole family decamped to Nymans, where there was another exciting new world to describe:

I wish you could see Nymans – you would be in ecstasies. The house and park and woods are lovely. The house is huge, about 25 bedrooms and dressing rooms and all furnished exquisitely with a scrupulous denial of anything verging on display or luxury. Only one bathroom in the house! and no gas or electric light. I have 12 candles to light my bedroom and the bath is brought in in the morning with huge jugs of hot water. Harold's father showed me most of the grounds the first day and I was enchanted. Such beautiful landscape gardening and views over miles of rolling country but alas no sun. Nothing but fog and rain, rain and fog! How I long for New York weather.

The Christmas season was very busy, with masses of presents, and Leonora was quite embarrassed by the consideration shown her. There were charades and impromptu theatricals in the evenings, and skating on the lake by day. The only defect was the dreadful cold: 'England is charming, but they don't heat the houses. Now I have chilblains, which are horrid,' she wrote, and later, after visiting another country house: 'American cold, even below zero, is nothing to the innate chill of an English house in winter. The manner of heating – more literally non heating! is depressing.'

Most of the family were probably gathered together at this Christmas party but Leonora's sister-in-law, Lennie's wife Maud, remained in London awaiting the birth of her third child. Harold must have talked a lot about Maud, as his bride was determined not to be quite put in the shade. In January 1904 she wrote to her mother:

Maud Messel, 1902

By the way I have not told you about the exquisite Maud, the essence of refinement and extravagance. She wears creations that impress one as being childishly simple and unpretentious until one realises how elaborate this sort of simplicity is. She is a perfect hostess, has beautiful manners and *savoir-faire*; both her houses are dreams of artistic furnishing and she is a marvellous housekeeper. But just about half an inch deep and after an hour utterly inane. She is fed on flattery from morning till night and cannot live without it. She is expecting a child now (today in fact) and her costuming for the occasion was wonderfully clever.

Leonora's criticism was rather sharp: although Maud's education had been somewhat limited she was by no means stupid. Her most priceless gift was her ability to inspire adoration; those outside the family were sometimes repelled by her languid airs and gushing manner but her sympathy and support for those who came within her magic circle were legendary. Those closest to her were perpetually showered with loving attentions while anyone who had befriended her in childhood, or any relative who had fallen on hard times, was always helped – not just with money, but with carefully chosen gifts and treats.

It is likely that Leonora modified her view, since over the next decade she and Harold were frequent guests at Balcombe House. Her brother-in-law she liked at once: 'Lennie is a good fellow and has been most charming to me. He has met me several times to go about and look for old furniture. I appreciated this as he knows such a lot about it.' Leonora's mother came to England in March and thereafter settled in Paris, visiting her daughter at regular intervals. These early letters are the only ones to survive.

Maud and Lennie's second son, Oliver, was born in London on 13 January 1904, the only one of their three children to inherit the Messel complexion. ('Very Hebrew looking' was the verdict of his grandmother Sambourne.) The house in Gloucester Terrace was now considered too small, so Lennie purchased 104 Lancaster Gate, directly overlooking Hyde Park. The children, however, spent most of their time in the country and all retained the happiest memories of their upbringing at Balcombe. Anne and Oliver grew up inseparable, united in their devotion to that 'perfect being', their mother Maud. Their father they admired from a distance; a charming and erudite figure to his contemporaries, capable of great kindness and generosity, he was intolerant of childish ways and all members of the household feared his sudden violent rages.

Lennie's youngest sister, Muriel, played an important part in the story of Nymans. In the Messels' early days at Westbourne Terrace when the nursery was full of children, Ludwig had scarcely concerned himself with his daughters; they feared rather than loved him and Ruth in particular seems to have felt neglected. She was fifteen when Muriel was born and quickly determined that this adored baby sister should be noticed and admired. At Nymans Ludwig could relax, shed some of his formality and enjoy walking round the garden; here the children played and Ruth saw to it that Muriel was often in her father's field of vision. Her strategy worked admirably: Ludwig suddenly discovered the charm of an intelligent, eager little girl and this youngest child was to become the darling of his old age.

Muriel grew up knowing every corner of the garden. She followed her father round when he talked to Comber, learning the names of the plants and where they came from, listening to discussions about which one should qualify for the most sheltered spot and which might grow huge and need more space. Playtime was often practical gardening and Muriel soon knew how to plant and prune and train. On the Messels' regular spring tours to Italy or the south of France, she would go with her father to look at gardens there which were full of lovely things. At home again they would walk round their own acres with fresh enthusiasm, wondering where space could be found for more treasures.

By the time she was in her teens Muriel was quite an expert in her

The herbaceous border, with a sundial in the centre, taken some time before 1909

own right. It is not known when she became responsible for a major task, the planting of the herbaceous borders in the orchard, but they may have been her special preserve from their inception. A tradition exists in the family that Muriel planned and planted the borders under the direct tuition of William Robinson. This is quite possible: a crusty old bachelor whose plain speaking roused animosity in many hearts, Robinson's most attractive characteristic was his love of children. He took a great interest in the education of young people, constantly encouraging them to appreciate everything beautiful in nature. In Muriel Messel he would have found a most receptive pupil.

Muriel would also have been greatly influenced by the work of Gertrude Jekyll. Miss Jekyll was already an experienced gardener when she first submitted articles to Robinson's magazine *The Garden* in 1875; her famous collaboration with Edwin Lutyens did not begin until 1889. Although she is believed to have come to Nymans to give advice in the early days there is unfortunately no evidence to prove the case. After 1907 she seldom moved from her home at Munstead Wood in Surrey, often drawing up plans for gardens which she never saw. Her precepts could of course be absorbed from her writings, as she published numerous books and articles which did as much as William Robinson's had done to change the way people thought about plants and gardens. The herbaceous border was her speciality and it quickly became the new status symbol for the country house. Such a border was – and still is – a real test of horticultural knowledge and skill, much more demanding than the old-style bedding-out. It is, however, almost as ephemeral; plants must be moved and divided every few years and without plans (such as Gertrude Jekyll always made when asked to create a garden from scratch) continuity is difficult.

Whatever it was that Muriel created – and she may have tried various schemes – it no longer survives. Only the tradition of a colourful summer border remains, and successive gardeners at Nymans have felt free to plant whatever they think best. Today a few clumps of perennials give solidity and backing but most of the plants used are hardy or half-hardy annuals in a gay mixture; the favourite Jekyll colour scheme of pale shades at each end of the border and fiery colours in the middle is not followed.

The first public indication that Nymans was developing into an unusually interesting garden came from an article in the magazine *Garden Life*, published on 5 August 1905. Entitled 'Famous Gardeners at Home (No. 200)' it gives an excellent idea of how much had been achieved in the ten years since James Comber had been appointed Head Gardener.

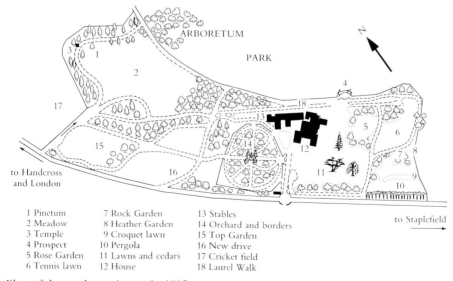

1 Pinetum	7 Rock Garden	13 Stables
2 Meadow	8 Heather Garden	14 Orchard and borders
3 Temple	9 Croquet lawn	15 Top Garden
4 Prospect	10 Pergola	16 New drive
5 Rose Garden	11 Lawns and cedars	17 Cricket field
6 Tennis lawn	12 House	18 Laurel Walk

Plan of the garden as it was in 1905

The magazine's reporter, accompanied by Comber, began his tour in the kitchen garden. This was the most labour-intensive part of any estate and where the head gardener's reputation mainly rested; more garden manuals existed on the growing of fruit and vegetables than anything else. Nymans seems to have had a good range of glasshouses: two vineries (early and late) produced magnificent crops, as did the two peach houses. The early peach trees, planted in 1896, were 18 feet tall and the fruit was, as Comber told the reporter, 'Well up to exhibition standards'. Another house contained strawberries; there was a fig house, a melon house, and a tomato house, while greengages, plums and figs were trained along the garden walls, one fine old specimen of 'Brunswick' fig having a span of 33 feet. In addition to the walled garden there was quite a large area surrounded by hedges where soft fruit and vegetables were grown. The reporter noticed several interesting new shrubs planted out in this sheltered place, *Carpenteria californica* and *Olearia nitida* (now *O. arborescens*) among others, which Comber told him were likely to prove too tender for the main garden.

A brisk walk round the pleasure grounds followed. The reporter was especially impressed with the Heath Garden: '"It was designed", said Mr Comber, "by Mr Messel, who takes the utmost interest in his gardens, and often assists me with his advice. We had no plan, but I got

Looking south across the lawn, with the Heath Garden and Pergola in the distance *c.* 1910. Ludwig can be seen with one of his daughters

it out to scale, and, Mr Messel having approved, we carried out the idea together".' From there they went to inspect the pergola and the rockery, then across the lawn to the Rose Garden (where the Sunk Garden is now). Here the beds were full of Hybrid Teas (most of the varieties Comber named are not grown nowadays) and climbing roses on poles, among them the latest witchuraiana hybrids. Then, after a brief look at the conservatory and 'the creepers on the mansion' the pair went into the 'new orchard' on the north side of the house. Here, apart from a passing mention of 'a noble herbaceous border, a hundred yards long and twelve feet wide', the talk was all of fruit.

Comber and the reporter then crossed over a drive which had been constructed the previous year to make a better approach for the house. Here was a lavish new planting of flowering trees and shrubs: one hundred *Magnolia stellata*, thirty cherries (the new 'James H. Veitch'), thirty-six *Cistus praecox*, thirty-six *Prunus triloba* and fifty double-flowering sloe, all in tight groups. The effect of this bold design would not become apparent for some years yet, so Comber and the reporter walked on to the Pinetum which was by now nicely established. It was clearly looking very handsome, as it merited several column inches in the magazine. There were at least fifteen different varieties of *Pinus*, fourteen *Thuja*, five *Sequoia*, seven Cedars, ten Junipers, five *Cryptomeria*, six *Retinospora*, twelve *Cupressus*, eleven *Tsuga*, as well as many others. After commenting favourably on the way the trees had been set out to maximum advantage, the reporter descended the hill to the lily pond (now gone) where twenty-three different types of *Nymphaea* were in excellent health. He and Comber did not continue their walk right down to the lake, nor go into the new arboretum, but Comber described an experiment being made there with a planting of nine species of eucalyptus. The pair then returned along the back drive, past beds of *Rhododendron hirsutum*, Scotch roses, kalmias and spiraeas, to the head gardener's cottage. After answering questions about his career before he came to Nymans, Comber finished by saying, 'We do not show, but we keep on making improvements and do the best we can to render all departments of the garden attractive.'

This tour took place in the summer, when the early flowering trees and shrubs, for which Nymans was later to be most celebrated, were not in bloom. Probably the collection of these was not yet extensive (certainly nothing of this sort seems to have been worth noticing in the orchard), but the magnolias and cherries along the drive and the unusual shrubs being nurtured in the kitchen garden must have marked the beginning of Ludwig's interest in such things.

Chapter Four

Plants and Plant Hunters

Fashions in gardening change all the time. The great loves of the mid-Victorian estate owner were coniferous trees, greenhouse plants, bedding-out and 'rock work'; in the latter half of the nineteenth century flowering shrubs, especially rhododendrons and azaleas, became all the rage. These splendid plants needed a mild damp atmosphere and rich acid soil to flourish best. The west coast of England, and parts of Scotland (where so many English landlords took their sporting holidays) made ideal habitats, but favourable conditions could also be found in the wealthy southern counties. A good display of rhododendrons became so much a mark of social respectability that late-Victorian tycoons made sure the soil was right before they purchased an estate: gardeners unfortunate enough to live on chalk or clay were in despair.

The British Isles have no native species of rhododendron. The 'wild' mauve *Rhododendron ponticum*, so common in woodlands today, comes from the Levant and was introduced to this country in 1763. *R. maximum*, the first of the American species to be imported, arrived in 1736 but was a disappointment, both in habit and flower colour. *R. caucasicum*, from Russia, which first flowered here in 1808, was a low, compact grower with flowers which varied from pale cream to yellow or pink. *R. catawbiense*, another American, flowered in 1813. It was not spectacular in colour but had a good habit and was extremely hardy. Experiments in hybridising with these four species were soon under way but the results were not very showy. However the scene changed dramatically when the first Himalayan species, *R. arboreum*, was brought to England in 1811, producing its striking bright red flowers in 1825. Although very tall and rather tender it was to be of great importance in the creation of colourful hybrids and some of the earliest of these are still worthy of a place in the modern garden. Deciduous rhododendrons – generally known as azaleas – were highly prized for their vivid orange and yellow colouring. Important early finds were *R. calendulaceum* (introduced from America in 1806) and the Russian *R. luteum* (1793) a parent of the famous 'Ghent' strain of azaleas raised in Belgium. Even if no further species had been discovered, rhododendrons and azaleas were, by the middle of the century, the finest flowering plants available for the large garden.

In 1847 Joseph Hooker (who was to succeed his father, William Jackson Hooker, as Director of the Royal Botanic Gardens, Kew, in 1865) set off on an important plant-hunting expedition to the Himalayas. His rich haul included forty-three new rhododendron species, one of which was *R. griffithianum*, thought by many enthusiasts to be the loveliest of all. Unfortunately, high-altitude plants (which in their native habitat do not put forth new growth until the snows have melted) find the vagaries of the English climate hard to bear; mild damp winters followed by severe spring frosts play havoc with emerging buds. Hardiness was all-important for commercial success and another plant hunter, Robert Fortune, had been to China, where climatic conditions more resembled those found in England, in 1843. From this and other journeys he brought back many splendid hardy plants; among those which grace our gardens today are *Anemone japonica*, *Jasminum nudiflorum* and *Dicentra spectabilis*. Fortune also found several rhododendrons, later-flowering and less tender than any of Hooker's introductions. One of these, collected in 1855, was named *Rhododendron fortunei*.

Robert Fortune's first journey to China was made under the aegis of the Horticultural Society of London. This had been founded in 1804 and was granted a Royal Charter in 1861. In spite of much good work and a few notable successes, financial mismanagement dogged its progress until Sir Trevor Lawrence became President in 1885. Under his guidance the Royal Horticultural Society not only became solvent, but steadily increased in prestige, running a demonstration garden in Chiswick (and for a time in Kensington also) and holding meetings and lectures on a regular basis. Fortnightly shows of flowers, fruit and vegetables took place in a small hall close to the Society's offices in Victoria Street, Westminster. The main public event, quite a feature of the London Season, was the annual Flower Show, which was held in the Temple Gardens from 1888, removing to Chelsea in 1913.

Sir Edmund Loder of Leonardslee was a staunch supporter of the RHS. A Member of Council since 1885, a keen raiser of unusual plants

– which were often shown at the Society's meetings – he no doubt urged his friends to join. In those days it was not a question of merely paying a subscription: Fellows (as members were then called) had to have sponsors and be formally elected, as with other learned societies. In May 1888 Ludwig Messel was elected to the Society and it seems quite likely that Sir Edmund was one of his sponsors. Ludwig does not appear to have taken an active part in proceedings, but he subscribed generously when an appeal was launched to enable the Society to move to better premises. Enough money was raised to build a fine large office block in Vincent Square with a splendid exhibition hall attached, which was opened by the King in July 1904. A new demonstration garden at Wisley was acquired the same year, so the Society was able to celebrate its centenary in fine style. As a result of all this enthusiasm and activity, membership rose from just over a thousand in 1888 to nearly ten times that figure twenty years later.

At Vincent Square the fortnightly shows became an oasis of delight for ordinary Londoners and a mecca for keen gardeners. Leading nurserymen took stands on a regular basis, while both amateurs and professionals competed in the various classes. Prizes and medals were awarded for large exhibits, and individual plants could be entered for the Society's special awards: the First Class Certificate (for plants of excellence) and the only slightly less prestigious Award of Merit were much coveted. Here a learner could pick up many useful hints, meet the erudite and famous, and aspire to great things himself.

The search for new and better strains of plants was a hobby taken up by many gardeners and estate owners. The demand for rhododendrons seemed insatiable and nurserymen, who depend on novelty for much of their business, had set to work with a will upon the material brought back by Hooker and Fortune. Within two decades more than five hundred different hybrids had been raised, named and distributed. By no means all were good (both form and colour have to be considered) and few were really hardy. The principles behind the creation of hybrids were not fully understood and a crop of two thousand seedlings, lovingly nurtured, might produce only one worthy new-comer. Thus it was that amateur enthusiasts with an eye for a good plant, as well as plenty of time and money to spare, were to make some of the greatest contributions to the marvellous range of hardy hybrid rhododendrons available in our gardens today.

The beautiful *Rhododendron griffithianum* had proved too tender for outdoors but the quality of flower was such that hybridisers were most anxious to incorporate it into their breeding programmes. In Sussex

Frederick Godman had a splendid example growing in his greenhouse at South Lodge, and in 1901 he invited his neighbour to come over to see it in bloom. Sir Edmund Loder took pollen from this plant and applied it to the flowers of a particularly fine form of the hardy *R. fortunei* growing in his garden. Several seedlings from this cross first flowered in 1907 and the original plants – now tree-sized – can still be seen at Leonardslee. A sensation at the time, with beautiful large flowers in white or shades of pink, frost resistant, *Rhododendron* 'Loderi' is acknowledged to be one of the best hybrids ever raised, a milestone in the history of rhododendron breeding.

Another famous hybrid is 'Loder's White'. This is the result of a different *Rhododendron griffithianum* cross (other parent unknown) and was one of a batch of seedlings raised by J.H. Mangles and sent by him to Frederick Godman. The plants were expected to be tender so Godman kept them under glass until they grew too large, whereupon he gave cuttings of a particularly promising white-flowered form to Sir Edmund. Grafted onto *ponticum* stock at Leonardslee and planted out in various positions, this soon proved to be hardy and Sir Edmund was able to distribute both 'Loder's White' and named forms of 'Loderi' to all his friends.

Edmund Loder's younger brother Gerald (fifth son of Sir Robert Loder) was the second member of the family to make his mark in the horticultural world. Called to the bar in 1888, Member of Parliament for Brighton from 1889 to 1905, he looked for an estate in Sussex where he could put some gardening ideas into practice. In 1903 he bought Wakehurst Place. A typical mid-Victorian layout with lawns and fine trees already existed here, but Gerald Loder greatly extended the collection of exotics, concentrating especially on rhododendrons and conifers. Taking his inspiration from Leonardslee he landscaped another valley garden, different yet equally magnificent. One of its most remarkable features was the 'Himalayan Glade' where plants from that region flourished as well as in their native habitat.

Wilfred Loder, of The High Beeches, died in 1902. His son, Giles, was only eighteen years old when he inherited the property, but he was a born gardener; with the encouragement of his mother he soon began extensive planting. Like his uncles, Giles Loder had a valley site to play with and a similar urge to create a new kind of romantic and colourful landscape deep in the heart of English woodland. Although The High Beeches is the smallest (and least visited) of the three Loder gardens, it uses almost identical material and is the very quintessence of the 'Sussex style'. Here, remote from the bustle of everyday life, glorious colour combinations unfold throughout the year, with May perhaps the most beautiful month: under a freshly emerging pale green canopy of native oak and beech, waxy magnolias, glossy-leaved camellias and sprawling rhododendrons dazzle the eye in every shade of pink and crimson, a sea of English bluebells at their feet.

Not far from Leonardslee was the garden of J. G. Millais, son of the famous artist John Everett Millais. Born in 1865, he was a little younger than Edmund Loder and Frederick Godman but shared their interest in foreign travel, big game hunting and every kind of wild life. He was also an accomplished artist and published several illustrated books on birds and mammals. In 1900 he built a house near Horsham, over-looking St Leonard's Forest, which he called Compton's Brow. When ill health prevented further travel, Millais' mind turned to gardening and he began to specialise in early-flowering shrubs, especially magno-lias and rhododendrons. He soon became an expert and was welcomed into the Loder circle. He and Sir Edmund often met to discuss gardening problems and to compare their wild life collections: Loder had quantities of horns, heads and animal skins, trophies of his hunting days, at Leonardslee, while Millais made a collection of 14,000 stuffed birds and mammals at Compton's Brow.

Millais greatly enjoyed visiting other gardens. His friendliness and enthusiasm created valuable links between their various owners and led to a pooling of their resources. He was frequently at Nymans, both in Ludwig's time and after the war: Comber and the Messels benefited greatly from his good advice. By 1905 Ludwig had begun his own collection of rhododendrons, both species and hybrids. The genus is vast and although over the years more space at Nymans was devoted to rhododendrons than to any other single plant family, the representation was never complete. Some eighty species and more than fifty named hybrids were growing there when a count was taken in 1916, and many more were added later. Comber made his own experiments too, grafting or striking cuttings given by friends and crossing various species, but as his master remained averse to the show-bench these efforts received no publicity.

Millais published the first volume of an important monograph on rhododendrons in 1917. This contained a list of Sussex gardens with fine collections, ending with South Lodge and Nymans: the author commented, 'the two last named are in fact among the best gardens in England'.

Although rhododendrons are the shrubs most frequently associated with the second half of the nineteenth century, they are of course only

James Comber and ten garden staff *c.* 1910. Note the oldest member, 'Dad' Jarvis, on Comber's left

one part of the garden story: throughout this period a stream of fine plants from all over the world was being imported to Europe. The Far East was the least explored and most tantalising for collectors: botanists were convinced that many good things were still awaiting discovery. Robert Fortune set out on his last expedition to China in 1860; John Gould Veitch went to Japan (which had only recently been opened to Europeans) the same year, and Charles Maries, also employed by Veitch, did some collecting in these parts also. But travel here had always been dangerous and difficult, often expressly forbidden by the authorities: thus it was French missionaries, working all their lives among the Chinese people, who had the best opportunities to gather new material. During the 1870s and 1880s David, Delavay and Farges, followed a little later by Soulié, sent home many good plants which later became disseminated to British gardens.

In 1880 Augustine Henry, an English official in the Chinese Customs Service, was posted to the remote upper reaches of the Yang-tse Kiang. To relieve loneliness and boredom he began to study botany, and sent a quantity of dried plant specimens to Kew. These aroused great interest in horticultural circles and Messrs Veitch decided that the time had come to mount another expedition to China, properly organised and headed by a trained collector. Ernest Wilson was the man chosen for the task and his first journey, which encompassed dangers and hardships of all kinds, lasted from 1899 to 1901. It resulted in a splendid haul, of trees and shrubs especially, and Wilson was so enamoured of China and its flora that he set out again in 1903, returning two years later with many more treasures.

Wilson's exploits in China had a most stimulating effect on gardeners in the West. At Nymans, the Messel–Comber partnership already had a bias towards woody plants, and within a few years of the article in *Garden Life* more lavish plantings of trees and shrubs were being undertaken. Like all enthusiasts, Ludwig soon eschewed the commonplace and concentrated his attention on all things new, or rare, or difficult, determined to prove that many lovely things could thrive in England, even on his windy Sussex hilltop. It was already apparent that the garden was surprisingly less cold than others only a mile or so away. Icy north-easterlies took a heavy toll, but with each year that passed the sheltering trees grew taller, the hedges thicker, and more tender plants were able to survive hidden in the lee of bulkier shrubs. Obsessed with gardening, Ludwig bought recklessly – almost, it would seem, all the plants that Veitch, or any other nurseryman, could offer. The enclosed orchard plot was the warmest and most sheltered part of the garden, so it was here that places were found for the cream of the collection. Rare trees (that would in time grow to record size) were underplanted with smaller shrubs; these in turn sheltered primulas, meconopsis, and lilies of all kinds. The walls provided different aspects to suit a multitude of climbing plants, some tender, some hardy, while roses and clematis were allowed to scramble through the apple trees. Everything flourished in the rich loamy soil, astonishing visitors and delighting its owner with a mass of blossom.

This fertile area of ground was no longer primarily an orchard, so henceforth it was called the 'Wall Garden'. It became the very heart of Nymans and, in contrast to the lavish planting of exotics – encouraged to grow lush and unfettered as they would in the wild – the original simple layout was strengthened and enhanced. On the south side, near the house, a short curved double flight of steps with carved stone balustrade led up into the enclosure. By 1909 a fine large marble urn containing a fountain had replaced the original sundial in the centre and the group of four yews, now grown large enough to clip into dramatic shapes, became one of the most notable features of the garden. At the far end of the main path an arched exit was crowned by some charming

Muriel Messel in the Wall Garden, 1912

pieces of Italian sculpture, linked by a miniature pediment. In spring the east–west borders were crowded with colourful bulbs, while in summer herbaceous plants made a splendid display along the main axis. Whether anyone other than Ludwig himself had any hand in the overall design is not known, but the contrast of wild and strictly formal elements within the curiously irregular boundary (the plot has nine sides) is most effective. It is some time before the visitor grasps the shape of the enclosure and this confusion – possibly quite unintended – adds to the sense of mystery and romance which is one of Nymans' most attractive characteristics.

Within a few years the Wall Garden became overstocked and a new piece of ground to the north, called the 'Top Garden', was taken into cultivation. Even in this more open position, trees and plants which a less adventurous gardener would not have risked grew well. Experience proved that things often succumbed if they were exposed to harsh conditions when young: new glasshouses and a frameyard were constructed close to the Wall Garden so that valuable specimens could be nurtured in pots for the first few years of growth before being set out in their permanent positions. Each winter there might be bitter losses, but each summer there were triumphs when something never known to flourish out of doors burst into flower, even set seed.

Ernest Wilson continued to explore the Far East, going again to China in 1907 and 1910 and to Japan in 1914 and 1917. These later expeditions were undertaken, not for Veitch, but for the Arnold Arboretum near Boston, Massachusetts, whose Keeper, Professor Sargent, was most generous in distributing seed to English gardeners. Altogether Wilson introduced more trees and shrubs to the western world than any other plant-hunter. One of his most spectacular finds was the handkerchief tree, *Davidia involucrata*. Seeds had been sent to France in 1897 by the Abbé David but only one plant had been raised there: one of Wilson's specific instructions on his first journey to China was to find where the davidia grew. After much travail he was successful, and Nymans obtained a seedling davidia very early – one planted out in the Wall Garden in 1908 flowered in 1915 and is still alive today. Other important Wilson plants growing at Nymans before the First World War were *Clematis armandii, Deutzia longifolia* (the parent of many good hybrids), *Dipelta floribunda, Lonicera nitida* and *L. tragophylla, Ligustrum lucidum, Magnolia delavayi, Meliosma veitchiorum, Styrax hemsleyanum* (the whole genus *Styrax* thrives in the sandy loam here) and *Vitis henryana*. Several species of berberis, rhododendron and viburnum which Wilson either introduced, or found especially hardy forms of, were also grown, and his later expeditions brought many more good things.

Another collector who worked in China during the same period as Wilson was George Forrest. His best discoveries, obtained in mild damp areas, are not as hardy as Wilson's plants but are suitable for sheltered gardens. His first trip to the Yunnan and Salween regions, which lasted from 1904 to 1907, was financed by Arthur Bulley who had a fine garden in Cheshire. Forrest too was lucky to survive many perilous adventures, and returned undaunted to China for more plant hunting in 1910. His third expedition, from 1912 to 1915, was largely financed by J. C. Williams, of Caerhays in Cornwall, supported by a syndicate of other garden owners. Born in 1861, Williams (always known as 'J. C.' to his friends) was from an early age fascinated by natural history, and became one of the foremost gardening experts of his generation. He had inherited a good garden at Caerhays Castle from his father, and here he specialised in daffodils and early-flowering shrubs – camellias, magnolias and rhododendrons – all of which grew magnificently in the mild Cornish air. By 1906 he had already purchased a large number of Wilson's rhododendrons from Messrs Veitch, and *R. williamsianum* was named for him by the collector in 1908. Part of the sponsoring arrangement made with Forrest on his

1912 expedition was a bonus paid for every new rhododendron found. (In total Forrest collected over 300 new rhododendron species, of which *R. griersonianum* was to prove the most important for hybridising purposes.)

An enthusiastic raiser of new hybrids, J. C. Williams encouraged his friends to do likewise but to concentrate only on the best, discarding anything unworthy. He was most generous with his own plants and saw to it that any good forms grown at Caerhays were widely distributed. He had met Gerald Loder in 1881 when they were both undergraduates at Cambridge and kept up a friendship with him and Sir Edmund until the end of his life, exchanging visits and discussing plants. (This link between the families held firm in the next two generations, J.C.'s son Charles being the best friend of Sir Edmund's son Robert: he was made guardian of the infant heir to Leonardslee when Robert was killed in the Great War.) Through the Loder connection the Messels came to know J. C. Williams and several other Cornish gardeners: they visited Caerhays, and probably Lanarth too, where P. D. Williams (J.C.'s cousin) had a fine garden especially famous for its daffodils.

In 1911 Arthur Bulley, whose chief interest was in alpines and herbaceous plants, employed Frank Kingdon-Ward to go plant hunting for him in Western China. *Meconopsis betonicifolia* and a large number of *Primula* species were introduced into cultivation by Kingdon Ward, but his own special liking was for rhododendrons. On a later expedition he found the pale yellow *R. wardii*, a species which has passed its good characteristics on to many hybrids. In time a great many Kingdon Ward plants came to Nymans.

It was probably Comber's continuing friendship with the staff at Veitch's Coombe Wood nursery which led to Nymans' extensive collection, not only of Chinese but also of South American plants. The first plant-hunter to be employed by Messrs Veitch was William Lobb who had collected for them from 1840 to 1857, mainly in Chile and its offshore islands. He brought back much useful material: *Azara microphylla, Berberidopsis corralina* and *Embothrium coccineum* all did well at Nymans, the embothrium producing its startling orange-scarlet flowers in 1913, the first time it had been known to flower outdoors in Sussex. Escallonias also enjoyed conditions there, especially *E. exoniensis*, one of Veitch's hybrids. Fine specimens of *Eucryphia cordifolia* and *E. glutinosa* (then known as *E. pinnatifolia*) proved that this family, usually considered tender, was perfectly hardy in the south of England: they flowered splendidly at Nymans every August and fruited well.

Myrtus luma and *M. ugni* also flowered freely, and although *Crinodendron hookerianum* was tender in the open, it did well when planted in a sheltered spot.

A wide selection of plants from the antipodes was also planted at Nymans. *Eucalyptus gunnii* and *E. coccifera*, raised from seed in 1905, suffered badly in the winter gales but acacias were more successful. Although *Acacia dealbata* was often cut back by frost, young shoots soon replaced the withered branches and it flowered freely in mild winters. New Zealand is the home of a great tribe of shrubby veronicas, now known as hebes: twelve species as well as a large number of hybrids grew well at Nymans. Olearias (like the hebes, on the borderline of hardiness) flourished without protection and thirteen species were listed in 1916; there were also nine species of leptospermum and eleven of grevillea. William Travers (1819–1903) is the collector associated with many New Zealand introductions: his son Henry corresponded with the Messels and sent several interesting plants directly to them. *Myrtus bullata* and *Hoheria populnea* came from him, and so probably did *Metrosideros lucida* which flowered at Nymans in 1914 (the first time it had been known to do so in England), thus meriting a photograph and description in the *Gardeners' Chronicle*.

Another source of plants was from the Messels' own travels. They had a winter holiday every year, either in the south of France or some other Mediterranean region, and several things were noted as coming from La Mortola, the fine garden owned by Sir Thomas Hanbury at Ventimiglia on the Italian Riviera.

Although the summer border in the Wall Garden, with the crown-shaped yews grouped round the fountain, is now the most photographed and easily recognised part of Nymans, it was not this which made Ludwig Messel's reputation. The layout of his Heath Garden was greatly admired and copied, the mass planting of magnolias and cherries by the drive was a spectacular success, but Nymans' special contribution to the horticultural world was its owner's willingness to experiment. Only a wealthy man could countenance the number of expensive losses which were incurred when plants of unknown hardiness were exposed to British weather conditions: Ludwig's reward was that Nymans became one of the best showcases in England for exotic plants. But the garden was never merely a gathering-together of rarities: each tree and shrub was placed with such sensitivity that all seemed natural and unforced. The beauty of the garden as a whole was paramount, every vista carefully considered as part of a chain of garden pictures. Ludwig Messel possessed imagination and a true artist's eye: he could play with form and colour in new and striking ways. Both as innovator and as visionary, he was respected by those gardening experts whose opinions he most valued.

Embothrium coccineum

Chapter Five

Gardening Friends

I n 1912 Ludwig began to keep a visitors' book at Nymans. From the names inscribed there it is apparent that an ever-widening circle of knowledgeable friends was convinced that a garden of outstanding interest was in process of creation. Some of them, like the Williams cousins and Arthur Boscawen (whose garden at Ludgvan was known as 'the Cornish Kew'), were expert in raising tender early flowering shrubs; their advice on what might be worth attempting to grow in colder, windy Sussex would have been invaluable. Arthur Dorrien-Smith of Tresco Abbey was another frequent visitor. His garden on the Scilly Isles, warmed by the waters of the Gulf Stream, more resembled the south of France than any part of England and was full of wonderful semi-tropical plants, the envy of all who had to contend with harsher climates.

One especially good friend and counsellor was Henry Elwes of Colesbourne Park, near Cheltenham. Elwes was another of that great band of Victorian gardeners whose early passions had been travel and sport. (His sister was the first wife of Frederick Godman and the two men remained life-long friends.) On his journeys around the world Elwes had turned to plant-hunting and was responsible for introducing dozens of new species to cultivation. His garden at Colesbourne became famous for its remarkable collection of rarities, with bulbous plants – lilies, crocuses and nerines – a speciality. Augustine Henry, retired from work in China, also visited Nymans; he collaborated with Elwes on a monumental work, *The Trees of Great Britain and Ireland*, the first volume of which came out in 1906. William Jackson Bean of Kew Gardens (author of *Trees and Shrubs hardy in the British Isles*) came often; other visitors were R. Irwin Lynch from the Botanic Garden, Cambridge, and R.L. Harrow from the Royal Botanic Gardens, Edinburgh. When L. and R. Chenault, well-known nurserymen of Orléans, came over from France in 1913 to tour English gardens, Nymans was on their itinerary.

Closer to home was Stephenson R. Clarke, another keen naturalist and sportsman. His wife was a niece of Frederick Godman and the couple had bought Borde Hill, a few miles east of Nymans, in 1893. Here again was an old house and garden set in extensive parkland, and at first only fairly conventional alterations took place. But by 1905 Stephenson Clarke had been swept up in the prevailing Sussex garden mania. He was especially inspired by Ernest Wilson's exploits in China and concentrated on making a comprehensive collection of flowering shrubs and trees from the Far East. Nymans and Borde Hill developed along very similar lines and a spirit of friendly rivalry sprang up between their owners which was to be continued in the next generation.

Arthur Soames was welcomed at Nymans too. In 1909 he bought Sheffield Park, Sussex, a big house designed by James Wyatt in 1775 for the third Earl of Sheffield. Part of the grounds had been landscaped by Capability Brown with a lake and clumps of trees, but Soames extended the park and added more water features. No doubt he consulted the Loders and the other established Sussex gardeners when he began planting. His site was less steep than theirs and the resulting landscape, with open views across the lakes, banks of flowering shrubs and groups of trees with varied leaf colour, is more reminiscent of Stourhead than Leonardslee.

A friend with slightly different interests was Alfred Parsons. One of the Sambourne circle, Parsons was a skilled watercolourist and botanical artist: he knew William Robinson well and spent several years working on the illustrations for Ellen Willmott's important book, *The Genus Rosa*. He also occasionally designed gardens and it is possible that he was responsible for some of the effects at Nymans. In July 1914 he was a guest of the Messels and painted a charming water-colour of the rock garden, which must have given his hosts great pleasure.

By 1914 all Ludwig's children had homes of their own, some having both a town house and a country retreat. Lennie's stucco-fronted six-storey house in Lancaster Gate was only slightly less imposing than his parents' London home nearby. It was, however, decorated in a much more modern way by the leading interior designers of the day, Lenygon and Morant, in what was called the 'Hampton Court Style'. The antique furniture had been carefully selected by Lennie from his favourite dealers, but the door handles, light fittings and other details were purpose-made to suit the chosen period. One room was designated a museum and lined with display cabinets: here Lennie kept his fine collections of china, early glass, fans and Japanese netsukes. In the country Maud's taste was more in evidence. Balcombe House had been built in early Georgian times and was furnished in keeping, the decorations – mostly pretty bits and pieces collected on foreign holidays – skilfully arranged against newly-fashionable plain white walls.

Lennie and Maud led a busy social life when they were in town but at least half the year was spent in the country, either at Balcombe House or holidaying elsewhere. Balcombe was their retreat from the world, a place to which only close friends were invited. These were often experts in the realm of antiques which Lennie loved to inhabit – Hugh Lane, Percy Macquoid, Archie Propert and many others. The writer Gladys Crozier was one of Maud's best friends, and the Messels liked to encourage young artists. Robert Brough, a follower of Sargent and tipped for a great career, came to Balcombe in the autumn of 1904 to paint Maud; only two months later he was tragically killed in a railway accident. In 1914 Glyn Philpot painted another portrait of Maud, as well as one of the two younger children, Anne and Oliver. They were ten and seven years old at the time and Philpot was in his mid-twenties,

Family and friends *c.* 1912. *Standing, left to right*: Bertie Gibbes, H.B. Hemming, Eric Parker, Cecil Winn, Arthur Gibbes. Seated: Ethel Bagge, Ruth Parker, Ottie Loring, Annie Messel, Hilda Gibbes, Ludwig Messel. *In front*: Charlotte and Dulcie Loring, Eric Parker junior

a charismatic figure who was to become Oliver's mentor in his subsequent career as an artist and stage designer.

Balcombe was about fifteen minutes' drive from Nymans along narrow country lanes. Lennie and Maud often went to visit Ludwig and Annie, to dine or spend the day, and when Marion Sambourne came to stay with her daughter and son-in-law her diary describes the busy comings and goings between the two houses. Each time she was taken over to Nymans there was at least one other set of children and grandchildren there, twenty-five people to lunch being not unusual. There would be much jollity, dressing up for charades, music-making and lively conversation, especially at Christmas, Ludwig's favourite time for gathering the brood together. By 1914 there were thirteen grandchildren: Lennie and Maud had three children, so did Ottilie and Ernest Loring. Ruth and Eric Parker had four (two more were born later), Hilda and Arthur Gibbes had one (another was born later), Harold and Leonora had two. As this last couple did not buy Danehurst, near Uckfield, until 1914, their offspring were often sent down to Sussex to enjoy the benefits of country air.

Those children who had Nymans as their playground in the golden years before the First World War were lucky indeed, surrounded by a close and affectionate family and backed by what seemed limitless prosperity. Victorian codes of behaviour were still enforced (fresh air, cold rooms, plain food and simple dresses were essential ingredients of nursery life) and children were expected to make their own amusements, not to bother the grown-ups. But they had the complete freedom of the garden and its surrounding woodland, and all grew up cherishing the memory of those happy times. Harold's son Rudolph had longer spells at Nymans than his cousins and it is he who, in a memoir written long after a new house had risen on the site, describes his grandparents' old home best:

The woods at Nymans were and still are extraordinarily beautiful. I remember so well the expanses of bluebell-covered ground, the golden carp in the lake and the graceful Greek temple overlooking the entrance to the woods . . . Nymans was a wonderful and lovable house. I shall never cease to regret the disappearance of the tower, the fantastic conservatory, the Greek porticoes and the heavenly Swiss chalet roof that covered the vast billiard room. We used to have tea under the portico, we played (on wet days) among Grandad's priceless plants in the conservatory and were allowed, but only on rare occasions, to climb the tower. The old Nymans was, I suppose,

Anne and Oliver Messel playing in the garden at Nymans

an architectural freak, but what a freak! . . . I was a morose and difficult child and remember retiring for long periods to the solitude of the billiard room where Grandad had installed an electric organ with a pianola attachment. There was a fine collection of rolls and I must have 'played' them all many times . . . Somehow no other house held for me the fascination of Nymans. I think my cousins, even though they had country houses of their own, will agree with me that there was nothing like the Nymans of our childhood.

Anne had memories too: of the rivalries and alliances between the cousins, the wonderful games of hide-and-seek (played in a garden which might have been designed for that purpose alone) and how each child in turn learnt to bicycle along the Laurel Walk. Anne had a natural affinity with plants and flowers: at home she arranged them with great flair and from an early age showed herself keen to master basic horticultural skills. A visit to Nymans was always a treat; although terrified of Comber (who naturally enough was not delighted to have hordes of children romping through his precious beds and borders), she subdued her fears in order to learn as much from him as she could. In later life she wrote, 'I can remember him making me spend a whole day tying and retying a wall plant in order to get the job perfect, reef knots and all. There was a reason why each thing had to be done, just so, and you had to learn it.' Comber might be a hard taskmaster but he was also an inspired teacher, greatly admired and respected by his employer, his colleagues, and the garden staff under him. Anne described him as 'One of the finest gardeners and most loyal of friends that a garden and a family could ever have.'

Anne also learnt a great deal from her aunt Muriel, who although only thirteen years her senior was an important force at Nymans. In 1914 Muriel was twenty-five and horticulturally very knowledgeable; her father was sixty-seven and by this time far from well. (Although the Messels continued to entertain, the Sambournes commented un-favourably on the pall of gloom – so unlike the former cheerful hospitality – which too often hung over Nymans during Ludwig's last years.) It was to Muriel that Ludwig increasingly turned for help and encouragement in his dealings with the garden.

Self-willed and impulsive as a child, Muriel had grown into a very modern young woman. Outspoken and thoroughly independent, she loved country life, kept her own horses and always had a dog at her heels. At a period when it was almost unheard of for a girl to own or drive a car, Muriel did both, behaving generally in a free and easy manner that charmed her many nephews and nieces. To them she was hardly an aunt at all, being far readier to join in their games and condone their naughtiness than the rest of the grown-ups. Like her brother Lennie she had a mercurial temperament which veered unexpectedly from high spirits to tantrums and sulks. She had a very different approach to life from her sister-in-law Maud, and each found the other tiresome and difficult, but Muriel's brothers and sisters were devoted to her: always known by them as 'the kid', she remained young at heart the whole of her brief life.

Muriel probably knew as much about the plants at Nymans, their provenance, date of planting and survival rate, as Ludwig or Comber did. In 1913 Sir Edmund Loder had published a list of everything growing at Leonardslee and he may have suggested to the Messels that they should do the same. During the last decade so much new material had come flooding in that there was a real risk of valuable information being lost: a systematic catalogue would be of inestimable use both to the garden owners themselves and for posterity. Comber had been making crosses and several of his hybrids were showing promise; other

Muriel Messel escorting her father round the garden *c.* 1914

plants were gifts from friends, of their own raising perhaps and as yet unproven. Many exciting things had been grown from seed and were botanically unclassified, their only identification a collector's number. Friends were consulted, experts from Kew were called in to advise and the compilation of the list – which Muriel was to call *A Garden Flora* – turned out to be more complicated and time-consuming than anyone had expected. Before the work was half complete war broke out, and Ludwig lost heart. Although he abandoned the project, Muriel soldiered on with what she came to regard as a sacred task, a memorial to her beloved father.

Many Englishmen accepted, long before 1914, that a major European war was inevitable. The unification of Germany under Prussia would not have pleased those natives of the Duchy of Hesse, Ludwig and Rudolph Messel. To them the ambitions of Bismarck and the loud-mouthed posturing of Wilhelm II would have seemed even more unpleasant and dangerous than they did to true-born Englishmen. Much of Ludwig's prosperity was based on investments in Germany and Russia, but due to the onset of ill-health he ignored all the warning signs. No alternative financial arrangements were considered, and when the war came his losses were enormous. But the real tragedy for the Messel family was that anyone having even remote connections with Germany became the enemy. Ludwig had relatives in Darmstadt; he himself never lost his strong German accent, and his loyalties were painfully divided. His children and grandchildren, who considered themselves utterly English, suffered too when they found themselves the targets of violent anti-German propaganda.

Fortunately Ludwig's sons were able to prove their patriotism in the best possible way. Since 1892 Lennie had belonged to the Volunteer movement and had spent much time at Balcombe drilling the local lads. Although debarred from serving overseas because of his German background, his valuable experience was much needed by the army and he was made responsible for raising and training the Fourth Reserve Battalion, The Buffs. He received the rank of Lieutenant-Colonel, a style of address which he kept for the rest of his life. Harold also served in the army and Muriel did splendid work nursing the wounded. But Ludwig sank into a deep depression; he died at Nymans in July 1915 of what his family always maintained was a broken heart.

Ludwig had made his will in 1910, when all seemed fair and prosperous. His widow was well provided for, with the use of both town and country house in her lifetime. Lennie was to inherit Nymans and become senior partner in L. Messel & Co. The big town house that

Ludwig and Annie had moved into a few years earlier, 3 Hyde Park Gardens, went to Harold. Several charities benefited and there were bequests of money to all his servants, both indoors and out, as well as for each employee of the firm. The residue was to be divided into eight shares, one for each child and one extra share for each of the sons. But alas, the war had changed everything and the residue – clearly expected to be very large – was almost nil. Lennie and Harold found themseves poorer than they had expected while the daughters (and their husbands) were grievously disappointed.

However, the firm was safe and Lennie at least did not appear to suffer great financial hardship. Now head of the family he was determined not to take the option, offered in his father's will, of selling Nymans to one of his siblings. (The property had been valued at £25,000 in 1910; one wonders what price it would have fetched in the lean years after the war.) At forty-three, Lennie was exactly the same age as his father had been when he purchased Nymans, twenty-five years earlier. Perhaps he wished, even more ardently than Ludwig had, to establish himself as a landowner in true English style. The big rambling house, with its marvellous views, the lands and woods and of course the garden, so much admired by all, would suit him perfectly. He decided to sell Balcombe House and move into Nymans at once.

To his surprise, Lennie met great opposition from his wife and children. They adored the home where they had lived so happily since 1904. Maud had perfected her own romantic style of decoration at Balcombe and although the house was not large, she had never wished for anything bigger. Nymans was a hideous Germanic folly – how could she arrange her furniture, or indeed her life, in such a setting? She wept bitterly at the thought of leaving; Anne and Oliver, always on their mother's side, begged their father to reconsider. But Lennie had his share of Messel obstinacy and would not budge, even though his sister Muriel also raised objections. She did not grudge Lennie's right to the house, but she could not bear the idea of his taking over the garden. He knew nothing about gardening and would ruin everything, she declared angrily.

At last a solution was found which, although it satisfied the new owners of Nymans, must have evoked a great deal of criticism from the other members of the family. Maud and Lennie took up residence in 1916 on the understanding that the old house, the fantastic creation of a quite outmoded way of thinking, would be pulled down. Maud would then decide what sort of mansion would rise in its place. However, there was still a war on, and rebuilding plans had to remain a dream for the next few years.

The garden naturally suffered during the war. Many of the staff were called up and Lennie was also away for much of the time. Comber, forty-eight when war broke out, was too old to enlist but he volunteered for Home Defence. At the same time he continued to hold things together at Nymans: both he and Muriel were able, albeit intermittently, to work on the list of plants growing in the garden. Visits from experts to authenticate the rarities must have provided welcome relief during the months when news from the Front was unbearably painful. Although there were no casualties in the Messel family itself, many of Lennie's close friends from his Eton and Oxford days were killed. Members of his father's circle were grief-sticken also: Sir Edmund Loder lost his only son, J. C. Williams two sons, Arthur Dorrien-Smith three.

In 1917 Muriel was able to arrange to have *A Garden Flora* published by *Country Life*. Over two thousand plants were listed alphabetically, with brief notes on some of the more remarkable species. These give planting dates and heights achieved in some instances, remarks on cultivation and hardiness in others. To later gardeners this list is of great historical value, but one cannot help regretting that the comments are not longer and more plentiful. It is particularly interesting to see which of the plants that were thought at the time to be tender have proved perfectly capable of standing up to even a harsh English winter. *Calceolaria integrifolia* was listed as a greenhouse plant, *Garrya elliptica* was set outside but still carefully protected, as were all types of fuchsia and most nothofagus. *Trachycarpus fortunei* and *Umbellularia californica* were also considered unsuitable for any but the most sheltered site.

Muriel wrote a short preface to her book, beginning with a brief description of the garden and then going on:

My most sincere thanks are due to all those who have so largely helped in the arranging of this list. They have, I know, done it 'in memoriam'. Mr Alfred Parsons has contributed ten illustrations of some of the most cherished specimens. Mr Robinson has written the introduction; Mr Bean has not only corrected the list but named numbers of plants which were wrongly labelled; Mr John Nix, too, helped greatly in the arrangement of the list, and James Comber, who planted the trees and shrubs, and has cared for them through more than twenty summers and winters, has supplied points of interest which otherwise would have remained unknown.

In her final paragraph Muriel wrote:

> I think that the garden may fitly be described as the triumph of hope.
> It was always full of experiments, it gave endless pleasure, and if you
> walk through it you will see the careful thought that was bestowed
> on each plant.

William Robinson's foreword begins:

> In L. Messel I had to deplore the loss of one of the most interesting
> garden lovers, a kindly thoughtful man with a genius for finding new
> ways in our garden trials and pleasures, who made himself a fair
> garden and made many experiments. We who think ourselves
> experienced as to what is worth testing have our limitations, and
> think we are wise in them, but he had none.

Robinson then mentioned some plants from distant parts of the earth
and went on:

> These trials of shrubs and rare trees were in what was once an old
> paddock near the house, protected by walls on north and east sides,
> and there one had the most instructive and in many ways beautiful
> results I have seen in a garden. On a May day it was a joy to see the
> way the Indian rhododendrons and many a choice shrub flowered,
> and there for the first time one saw the fine *Eucryphia cordifolia* and
> *Davidia involucrata* in bloom . . . What others considered difficult,
> Mr Messel at once wished to try, and was gratified when he
> succeeded in flowering such plants as *Hoheria populnea*, *Embothrium
> coccineum* and *Cestrum elegans* 'Newellii' in the open air.

Part II

NYMANS
AND
LEONARD MESSEL

Chapter Six

A New Generation

F or the Messel family the years from 1918 to 1920 were even more full of sorrow than the early part of the war. One crippling blow followed another: in May 1918 Harold's wife, Leonora, died giving birth to a stillborn child; on 1 December in the same year Muriel fell victim to the great influenza epidemic that killed more people in one winter than had perished in four years of battle. Harold never recovered from the loss of his wife and committed suicide in 1920, leaving his two children in the guardianship of their maternal grandmother, Mrs Gibson. Annie Messel, in poor health for several years, died at her London home on 7 December 1920. A tablet was put up in her memory in St James's Church, Sussex Gardens, where she had worshipped for forty years, and she was buried beside her husband in Kensal Green cemetery. Ludwig's brother Rudolph, who died in April 1920, also lies here.

Rudolph Messel was a brilliant chemist who devoted his life to the service of his adopted country. He was a partner in the chemical manufacturing firm of Spencer Chapman & Messel, and had himself invented a new process for manufacturing sulphuric anhydride, an important constituent of dyes and explosives. The improvements in explosives, used primarily for mining and engineering works all round the world, raised British prestige and brought substantial profits: Rudolph became a very rich man indeed. It must have seemed a bitter irony when his invention was turned to military use for the destruction of German enemies during the war. A Fellow of the Royal Society and a founder member (in 1881) of the Society of Chemical Industry, Rudolph left the bulk of his fortune to the furtherance of scientific research. The Messel Medal, instituted in his honour in 1921, is presented each year by the SCI to a person who has given distinguished service to science, literature, industry or public affairs. Rudolph never married, but was a welcome visitor at the houses of his brothers and sisters, his nephews and nieces always grateful for his jovial kindness and typical Messel generosity.

Ludwig's sister Eugenie had married a stockbroker, Eugen de la Penha, and this couple are also buried at Kensal Green (Eugenie died in 1908). Alfred, the third Messel brother, lived and worked in Germany until his death in 1909. His architectural career was very distinguished and some of his buildings, in the Art Deco style, still survive. In Berlin a grassy open space, Messel-platz, was named after him. The last survivor of this generation of the family, Lina Seligman, died in 1925.

The old aristocracy and landed gentry, whose financial difficulties and consequent loss of influence had begun fifty years earlier, were now staggering under the weight of crippling taxes but those whose wealth did not depend on agriculture continued their rise in the social firmament. Stockbroking was not much affected by the post-war depression and the firm of L. Messel did well in the 1920s and '30s. Lennie, now senior partner, had no real gift for financial dealing but he made an adequate figurehead; his other partners were quite competent, so that he drew a very comfortable income from the business. The succession was assured as his sons, Linley and Oliver, were expected to follow in his footsteps, as was Harold's son, young Rudolph. (Harold

Leonard Messel in middle age

had been the only one of the family to inherit Ludwig's magic touch with money and his early death was a great loss for the firm). Lennie had made a distinguished contribution to the war effort, for which he was awarded the OBE, and he was anxious to resume the life of a country gentleman. Now that his family were well settled in at Nymans he was determined to keep the garden up to the same standard of excellence as in his father's time.

Muriel had been wrong when she said that her brother knew nothing about gardening. Busy with his City career, he had not striven, as she had, to become an expert, but he did not lack interest in the subject. At the first country house he and Maud owned he had brought wild primroses into the garden, a very Robinsonian idea. When they moved to Balcombe House in 1902 it had parkland round it and a good kitchen garden but no flower garden, so Lennie worked hard to create one, although it was never as large or as fine as the garden at Nymans. Trees were cut down and scrub cleared to make room for a terrace, a rose garden and a rockery, but at that time it was probably Maud, not her husband, who decided what should be grown and where.

From her earliest days Maud had enjoyed picking flowers and distributing bunches to family and friends; to the end of her life she greatly valued plants and flowers, not for their rarity, but for their sentimental overtones, reminders of people or places that she loved. Her drawing-room was always filled with bowls of flowers, scented daphne and lavender from the garden, wildlings from the meadows, great branches picked from the hedgerow or the orchard. The soft-petalled, drooping, heavily-scented old roses – whose beauty lasted for a brief day only – exactly suited her romantic style. Ousted by new, vigorous, brightly-coloured cultivars, these roses were often neglected in turn-of-the-century gardens. At Balcombe Maud began to cherish them, finding an ally in that famous lady gardener, Ellen Willmott of Warley Place, Essex. Without Miss Willmott's championship and the devotion of a handful of enthusiasts (of whom Maud Messel was one), many of the old roses which we value today would have been lost to cultivation.

How long it took to kindle Lennie's passionate pride in the garden at Nymans, which became so evident in the ensuing years, is not known, but as soon as the war was over the staff was quickly brought up to full strength – in fact Comber found it easier to talk the new master into spending money on men and materials than he had the old. Lennie was only a few years younger than his head gardener; he had always respected Comber's expertise, and he responded eagerly to his suggestions. For the rest of his life he regarded him as a friend and colleague rather than an employee, and this new partnership was to be just as successful as that originally forged by Ludwig. Great things were to be done at Nymans in the next phase of the garden's development.

Lennie's approach to gardening was always that of a collector. From his youth he had been a connoisseur of rare and beautiful objects and by middle age he had no need to go shopping: art dealers from all over the world would come to his house to present their treasures for his inspection. Muriel's work on *A Garden Flora* would have opened his eyes to a new opportunity for specialisation: a catalogue was something he understood well, and it was always the number of different varieties of any one genus which could be grown at Nymans which fascinated him. Ludwig had already gathered together a vast collection of rare trees and shrubs of all kinds, but Lennie preferred to narrow the field by concentrating his attention on a few plant families. Rhododendrons were his greatest love and he continued to buy new species and to acquire hybrids. Later Nymans became famous for its magnolias, camellias and hydrangeas.

Maud brought her influence to bear also. Never an active gardener (she suffered from an arthritic back), gentle suggestion was her forte and the largely shrubby planting at Nymans was soon softened by the addition of the humble old-fashioned flowers and scented herbs which were her favourites. She had a special love for small bulbs and all the earliest harbingers of spring: drifts of snowdrops, snowflakes and *Cyclamen coum* (grown from seed collected by E. K. Balls in the mountains of Asia Minor) were to become a feature of the garden, a joyful sight in the coldest months of the year. Later erythroniums, blue scillas and crocus of all colours made bright carpets underneath the trees, with narcissus and primroses naturalised in the meadows. Although there were many roses at Nymans already the collection was greatly enhanced when Maud's favourites were brought over from Balcombe. Under her direction the old frameyard (with a well at its centre) north of the Wall Garden was remodelled and planted with old-fashioned roses.

Lennie himself had no eye for grand design; although he could appreciate the massed planting and the pictorial effects which made his father's garden so attractive he never felt the urge to do more of the same, so the outline of Ludwig's creation remained unaltered. The sheltering trees and hedges of holly and laurel had by now grown thick and sturdy; bitter winds were far less of a problem than they had been

in the early days, and spring especially was a time of heart-stopping
beauty. Twenty-five years since its planting, the Pinetum was looking
splendid and the Wall Garden too was well established. But inevitably
the character of the garden changed. Each year the trees cut out more
light, shrubs grew into each other, distant views were first blurred,
then quite concealed. Nymans was becoming more secret and secluded,
in Maud's eyes a far more romantic and beautiful place than the one she
remembered from her first visit in 1893. All she needed now was a
house which would complement the garden.

Lennie was quite happy to indulge his wife when reminded of his
promise to rebuild Nymans. Maud had abandoned her youthful
ambition for an artistic career when she married; now she eagerly
grasped the opportunity to draw again and made numerous sketches
for a dream house. Hers was a truly Romantic vision – a building with
its origins in the fourteenth century, perhaps a monastic foundation,
altered and added to by many generations until perfected in Elizabethan
times. It must be built of stone, with arched and mullioned windows,
steep pitched roof and tall chimneys. A Great Hall was essential, a long
drawing-room, fine library and staircase, perhaps a minstrel's gallery.
Every trace of the old façade must be obliterated, the only gesture
towards economy being the use of the original foundations. In fact
Maud was so firm in her ideas, so unwilling to compromise, that the
first architect the Messels employed, Raymond Evill, was driven to
resign at an early stage in the proceedings. He was replaced by Sir
Walter Tapper, an architect of some distinction who specialised in
churches and thus understood his client's medieval yearnings. But the
struggle was long and costly: a full five years passed before the new
house was finally completed in 1928. Even Lennie, who had endorsed
his wife's ideas and was very proud of the result, must have blenched a
little at the bill.

The ground plan of Nymans was actually altered very little; as in
Ludwig's time, the bones of the old building were merely given a new
skin. Much to Maud and Lennie's delight, genuine medieval stonework
was discovered on the west front, up to the tops of the ground floor
windows, and internally an ancient doorway was incorporated into the
new work. The main alteration was the approach to the house: this was
now from the east so that visitors could appreciate the view across the
valley before passing through an arched gateway into a small courtyard,
overhung with trees, on the south-east corner. From here a flight of
steps led up to the new front door; a dark entrance hall and 'screens
passage' opened dramatically into the double-height hall with its tall

Nymans rebuilt to designs by Raymond Evill and Walter Tapper. The south front, with the Great Hall on the right, 1932

traceried windows. Beyond this was the library and then the drawing-room, with beamed ceiling and huge log-burning fireplace. Above, on the south-west corner, was Maud's bedroom with an oriel window commanding the best view. In the west wing the old entrance hall became another living-room, its porch opening into a secluded walled garden which caught the afternoon sun. Planted with lavender and box, the layout here was simple but the stone-roofed dovecote in one corner is perhaps the most charming of all the garden's architectural features.

Soon after the new house was finished Christopher Hussey came to make a report on it for *Country Life*. Photographs were taken of all the rooms and these are of great interest because they show a style of interior decoration, the height of fashion at the time, which has not yet seen a revival. The new Nymans was greatly praised, both inside and out, for its skilful re-creation of an English manor house, complete with many genuine old beams, fireplaces and stone-carving purchased on the antique market. But to modern eyes the rooms look thoroughly uncomfortable. The Jacobean furniture, all knobs and curls, the board floors and whitewashed walls contrast sharply with the Victorian cosiness and clutter which is now back in fashion; the old Nymans, if it

The drawing room at Nymans, 1932

still existed, would find more favour today than Maud and Lennie's careful pastiche.

Although much of the Messels' time during the 1920s was taken up with the rebuilding of their house, it was the doings of their three high-spirited children, now entering adulthood, which had first claim on their attention. The eldest, Linley, reached his majority in 1920 and after leaving Cambridge satisfied his father's ambitions by joining the family firm. Anne, three years younger, was presented at court in June 1922. Small and lively, enchantingly pretty and indulged by doting parents with everything money could buy, she was soon surrounded by a host of admirers. The big London house in Lancaster Gate made an ideal base for several seasons of parties and dances for young people while Nymans was, as ever, the perfect weekend retreat.

In spite of a scanty formal education – a string of French and German governesses had not been inspiring – Anne was by no means empty-headed. Her father's expert connoisseurship exercised a lasting influence and she had an unerring eye for things beautiful and rare. From her Messel background too came a single-mindedness in the pursuit of any goal on which she had set her heart, and an abiding interest in plants and gardens which would in time, serve Nymans well. She inherited much from her mother: not only Maud's irresistible charm and impeccable dress sense, but also her deep devotion to the past. Any sentimental or romantic relic, every family letter, piece of handwork, *memorabilia* of any kind – no matter how old and faded – was always treasured and preserved.

Oliver, two years younger than Anne, defied all attempts to turn him into a stockbroker. He had hated Eton and did not, as his parents hoped, go on to university. Instead, he persuaded them to allow him to study art, and was enrolled at the Slade School in 1923. After a year there he became a pupil of Glyn Philpot, under whose influence he gravitated towards theatre design. His first exhibition in 1924, of theatrical masks made in papier mâché, was a success and it led to him being asked to make something similar for Diaghilev's ballet, *Zéphyre et Flore*, produced the following year.

Anne found Oliver's contemporaries – lively, stage-struck and hedonistic – more congenial than most of her suitors of more marriageable age. She was, however, quite willing to comply with her parents' hopes of a good match, and it was one of her elder brother Linley's friends, Ronald Armstrong-Jones, who eventually carried off

Mrs Ronald Armstrong-Jones
c. 1926

the prize. The son of a distinguished doctor knighted for his service in the field of mental health, Ronald had all the attributes of a suitable husband. Handsome, clever and rather serious, he had been called to the Bar in 1922 and was already making a name for himself. He was also a lover of all country pursuits, something which endeared him to the Messels, who welcomed him to Nymans. In fact he and Anne seemed to complement one another perfectly, solid worth against quicksilver charm, and both families were delighted with the match.

On 22 July 1925 the Messels gave their only daughter a splendid wedding. Anne wore a white satin dress embroidered with pearls; she was followed up the aisle of St Margaret's, Westminster, by eight bridesmaids and three child attendants in shaded cream chiffon with head-dresses and girdles of green leaves, costumes which bore the stamp of Oliver's emerging genius. The reception was held at Lancaster Gate and the young couple went abroad for their honeymoon. On their return they set up home at 25 Eaton Terrace, the gift of the bride's parents. Here Anne was able to make her first experiments in interior decoration: bright fabrics and pale walls set off many pretty *objets d'art* and carefully chosen pieces of eighteenth-century furniture. The little house made a charming background for the busy social whirl which Anne enjoyed so much. However, she did not desert Nymans, often spending weekends there, walking round the garden with her parents and sharing their enthusiasm while Ronald went shooting or fishing. As a wedding gift – in return for all the presents showered on her by her father – she gave Lennie something of inestimable value: a piece of neglected land just across the road from the entrance gate of Nymans. The main garden was already full to overflowing and when this new plot was cleared it provided space for thousands more exciting new plants.

In 1926 C. B. Cochran commissioned Oliver to design some masks and costumes for one of his famous revues. These were a spectacular success and at the first night the audience broke into spontaneous applause when the curtain rose. Oliver's theatrical career, which was to be long and distinguished, had got off to a flying start, and no one was more pleased and supportive than his sister Anne. Skilful with a needle, she helped make some of the costumes he designed for Cochran, as well as for the many charity matinées and fancy-dress balls which were a feature of fashionable London in the 1920s. It was at one such party (when wearing another of Oliver's creations) that she caught the eye of Cecil Beaton. He made several charming portrait studies of her and became a firm friend. Other photographers also clustered round and

Anne's admirers were delighted when pictures of her appeared in *The Tatler*, captioned 'One of the most beautiful women in Society, leader of the younger set and sister of Oliver Messel, the well known artist and stage designer'.

In 1927 a daughter, Susan, was born to Anne and Ronald at Eaton Terrace and a son, Antony, followed three years later.

Eucryphia cordifolia

Chapter Seven

The Garden Matures

L ennie was a shy man who had never aspired to cut a figure in public, but from the time that he established himself at Nymans he appeared to grow in confidence. He took great delight in showing off his treasures, both inside and outside the house, to anyone who was really interested. His father's gardening friends were entertained as before: J.C. Williams, Henry Elwes, Stephenson Clarke and his son Ralph, Johnny Millais, Arthur Dorrien-Smith and many others were always welcome at Nymans and left their signatures in the visitors' book. Frederick Godman had died in 1919 but his widow Alice and their two daughters, Eva and Edith, still came over regularly from South Lodge, where the fine garden was maintained as well as ever. Gerald Loder of Wakehurst Place and his brother Reginald (who had a beautiful garden at Maidwell Hall in Northamptonshire) were frequent guests at Nymans, as was their nephew Giles from The High Beeches. Sir Edmund Loder died in 1920, aged seventy-one, but Lady Loder kept a watchful eye on the garden during the minority of her grandson (also named Giles) who, in his turn, was to become a worthy keeper of the flame.

The Messels made new gardening friends too, and Lennie liked to arrange meetings between fellow enthusiasts. Two Gloucestershire gardeners, Mark Fenwick of Abbotswood and Lawrence Johnson of Hidcote Manor, were entertained together at Nymans in May 1919 and thereafter visited separately on many occasions. Frederick Stern and Lionel de Rothschild both came in May 1920; their gardens could not have been more different. Frederick Stern's at Highdown, Worthing, was largely created in a chalk pit where the thin alkaline soil was anathema to rhododendrons, camellias, magnolias and other fashionable plants. His book *A Chalk Garden* gave great encouragement to those who despaired of creating a landscape like Sheffield Park, or of making a collection of rhododendrons and their hybrids such as Lionel de Rothschild had recently begun at Exbury in Hampshire.

Other friends who inscribed their names in the Nymans visitors' book during the 1920s were Robert James from Richmond, Yorkshire (remembered for the climbing rose 'Bobbie James'), Frederick Balfour from Scotland (the 'Dawyck' beech), Hugh Armytage Moore from Rowallane, Ireland (home of many good plants), Edward James of West Dean, Sussex, E.A. Bowles of Myddleton House, Middlesex, and Reginald Cory of Duffryn, Cardiff, fine plantsmen all, quick to appreciate Lennie's ambitions for his garden and delighted to share their experiences. Maud was a wonderful hostess to these erudite gentlemen and their often very knowledgeable wives; she was also good friends with many lady gardeners who were recognised as experts in their own right. Ellen Willmott came to Nymans in August 1921 to discuss roses, Norah Lindsay (who was responsible for some of the planting at Hidcote and at Montacute) came in 1927. William Robinson's last recorded visit to Nymans was in May 1931. A fall in 1909 had put him into a wheelchair, but at ninety-two he was still indomitable. No doubt he enjoyed being pushed along the garden paths to admire his old friend's favourite plants in all their glory.

Encouraged by the enthusiasm of so many garden experts, Lennie decided to move closer into the orbit of the Royal Horticultural Society. The Great War had put a check on its activities but the shows had not been entirely abandoned and under the presidency of Lord Lambourne (1919 to 1928) the RHS entered a further period of expansion. Gerald Loder's garden at Wakehurst Place was reaching maturity and he was very active in the Society's affairs: elected to the Council in 1920, he presented the Loder Rhododendron Cup (in memory of his brother) in 1921. From 1924 he was on the judging committees for awards to trees, shrubs and botanical species, and must have encouraged all his friends to come to the fortnightly shows and if possible exhibit their plants. Sussex gardeners were particularly well placed for attending events at the RHS headquarters in Vincent Square (Victoria station being only five minutes' walk away), and during the early 1920s material from the gardens of Borde Hill and South Lodge began to be shown there, often winning top prizes. On 10 April 1923 a new exhibitor appeared: the name-card on a display of seedling rhododendrons read 'Lt.-Colonel L. C. R. Messel, OBE, Nymans, Handcross, Sussex'. A Silver Medal was won that day, much to the home team's delight, and a Silver Gilt one (again for rhododendrons) at the next show. On 8 May only one plant was sent up for the judges to assess: this was a particularly good form of *Rhododendron decorum*, named 'Mrs Messel' in Maud's honour. The citation described it as 'A very fine variety with broad open flowers of pure white borne in handsome trusses', and it was given an Award of Merit.

These triumphs on the show bench must have been especially pleasing for Comber, obliged for so many years to hide his light under a bushel. As a young man he had enjoyed exhibiting, and was particularly proud of several varieties of verbena which he had bred and which he always grew at Nymans. With so much new material coming to hand there were plenty of opportunities for experiment; in 1913 he had obtained a truss of *Rhododendron* 'Loderi' which he had used as a pollen parent. From various crosses with other varieties many promising seedlings were raised. In pre-war days there would have been little thought of distributing the results of such work to anyone other than a close friend: professional nurserymen used mail-order catalogues to advertise their own productions and only occasionally took up the work of an amateur. Ludwig had set his face against flower shows, but they were very popular events in country districts. Usually held in high summer in a marquee or village hall, they were the only way that most gardeners had of seeing or displaying anything new. The RHS's shows in London had two great advantages: they drew on expertise from a wider radius than the usual village or county show, and they were held at regular intervals right through the year. Thus many rare and beautiful plants were seen for the first time by the garden-loving public at Vincent Square and it was not surprising that those which flowered in spring or early summer often generated the most interest.

In September 1924 Lennie was asked to be one of the judges at the Society's Autumn Show, held that year in Holland Park, and in June 1925 the RHS instigated a special annual flower show for amateur exhibitors only. Nymans won a Silver Gilt Medal for a display of flowering shrubs that year, a Gold Medal (again for flowering shrubs) in 1927 and a Silver Gilt one in 1928. But perhaps the greatest excitement was caused by the success of a new *Eucryphia* hybrid, sent up to one of the regular shows in August 1925.

Eucryphias grew well at Nymans: fine specimens of *E. cordifolia* and *E. glutinosa* were now mature and seedlings were often found beneath the trees. *E. glutinosa* is usually the first to flower and is over by the time *E. cordifolia* opens, but sometimes their flowering seasons overlap. In 1914, after one such summer, Comber's sharp eye noticed that some seedlings looked a little different: the bees had been busy and a natural hybrid had occurred between the species. Potted up and carefully tended, two small plants (labelled A and B) survived to become healthy trees, apparently quite hardy. Great was everyone's delight when the first flowering indicated that they might surpass their parents in beauty. Eucryphias are very useful in the garden as they bloom in August, long after most flowering shrubs have finished their display: a new type would be a welcome addition to the late summer garden. While Comber was debating which one of his plants to take to the Society's August show, seedling B unaccountably died. 'Nymans A' was set before the judges but by accident the label was wrongly inscribed – the coveted Award of Merit went to *Eucryphia x nymansensis* 'Nymansay'. (A better name would have been hard to find!) In February 1926, at the Society's AGM, it received the Cory Cup for the best new hybrid of the year. (This prize had been instigated in 1923, to encourage the production of hardy hybrids of garden origin, by Reginald Cory, a member of the RHS Council for many years.) Two years later the Award of Merit for *Eucryphia* 'Nymansay' was upgraded to a First Class Certificate, only given to plants of 'great excellence'.

After being known for so long only to a select coterie of dedicated horticulturists, the names of the most innovative Sussex gardens – Leonardslee, South Lodge, Wakehurst Place, Borde Hill and Nymans – were becoming familiar to a wider public. In the twenty-five-year period between the two world wars there was seldom a show in Vincent Square at which at least one of this closely linked group did not exhibit and win prizes. (Most of them have continued, with only brief intervals, to do so up to the present day.) The stimulus of public competition was invaluable: in a spirit of friendly rivalry each strove to do better than the other, while collectively they fought off challenges from further afield. Foremost among contenders for prizes during this period were two other large private gardens of the same 'natural' type, both with a penchant for rhododendrons: Exbury, owned by Lionel de Rothschild, and Bodnant in North Wales, home of the Aberconway family.

Bodnant had been purchased in 1874 by Henry Pochin, a wealthy industrialist who devoted the rest of his life to improving his estate and planting an extensive garden. On his death in 1894 the property passed to his daughter Laura, the wife of Charles McLaren, a barrister and Member of Parliament who was created first Baron Aberconway in 1911. Lady Aberconway was an enthusiastic gardener who greatly increased the collection of plants at Bodnant and passed her love of flowers on to her son Henry. From the time that Henry McLaren left university in 1901 he shared the care of the garden with his mother, exhibiting at the RHS under their joint names until her death in 1933.

As well as being a great plantsman he proved a brilliant garden designer, supervising the construction of a series of magnificent formal terraces to the west of the house. He also continued the work begun by his grandfather in the sheltered valley of the little river Hiraethlyn, where a dramatic woodland paradise, similar in many ways to the Loder gardens in Sussex, was in process of creation. Like so many of his contemporaries, Henry McLaren was fascinated by the collecting exploits of Wilson, Forrest and Kingdon-Ward in the Far East. He acquired from them a vast number of new plants for his garden, with rhododendrons being perhaps his greatest love. An ardent supporter of the RHS, he became a member of Council in 1923 and was to exercise great influence over the Society's affairs. Not only did he subscribe to several plant-hunting expeditions himself but he urged the Society to do likewise, believing that their experimental garden at Wisley should strive to become the best in the world.

The first show at Vincent Square to be devoted entirely to the genus *Rhododendron* was held in 1926. It was arranged by the Rhododendron Society, an informal group of about twenty-five enthusiasts (J. C. Williams was one of the leading spirits) who had first banded together in 1915. Although this show was a great success Lionel de Rothschild suggested that a larger organisation, which could stage an even bigger show every year and issue more publications, was desirable. A meeting was called in 1927 at which he took the chair to found the Rhododendron Association; among the 114 members enrolled that day were Lady Aberconway, Henry McLaren, Gerald Loder, Johnny Millais, Leonard Messel and James Comber. Several professional nurserymen, among them Peter Veitch, Gomer Waterer and John Cheal, also joined. Over the next few years some valuable monographs on the genus were published and the annual Rhododendron Show became an important event in the floral calendar.

Lionel de Rothschild did not begin to garden at Exbury until after the war but then, with vast resources at his disposal, probably produced more fine rhododendron hybrids during the next quarter-century than any other amateur breeder. But this was a game anyone could play: Comber continued his own breeding programme and over the next few years Nymans sent many good new rhododendrons up to Vincent Square. These were named after members of the Messel family: 'Linley', and 'Oliver', both Loderi hybrids, won Awards of Merit during 1927, while 'Anne' and 'Linley Sambourne' (Maud's father) were successful in 1928. 'Muriel Messel', described in the citation as 'a hybrid of unusual charm . . . from bright pink buds expand well disposed flowers of exquisite shape and delicate colouring . . .' won an Award of Merit in 1929.

A cross between *Rhododendron decorum* 'Mrs Messel' and *R. griffithianum* produced several fine plants of which Comber was especially proud. As *R. decorum* is closely related to *R. fortunei*, the results superficially resembled *R.* 'Loderi' and were equally sweet-scented, but the flowering period was more extended. Two of the white hybrids, 'Susan' and 'Tony' (named after the Messel grandchildren), won Awards of Merit in 1930 followed by 'Madonna' in 1931 and 'Mrs J.Comber' in 1932. Although these flowered magnificently at Nymans for many years (during the 1930s they were a splendid feature of the garden) they were never taken up by the trade. Sadly, most of the fine rhododendron hybrids raised by Comber during his long life have been lost; storms, drought and general neglect during and after the Second World War all took their toll. One or two plants of 'Mrs Messel', 'Madonna' and 'Mrs J.Comber' have recently been discovered in the further parts of the garden and efforts are now being made to propagate these and thus preserve them for others to enjoy.

Gerald Loder, who succeeded Lord Lambourne as President of the RHS in 1929, had only a short spell in office, retiring in 1931. (Raised to the peerage in 1934 as Lord Wakehurst, he died in 1936, aged seventy-one.) He was much missed by his Sussex friends but the Society was fortunate in his sucessor, Henry McLaren. Like Loder, McLaren led a busy public life as a Member of Parliament and chairman of several important companies, but he still found plenty of time to devote to his own garden at Bodnant and to the affairs of the wider gardening public. In 1934 he inherited the title of Lord Aberconway and he was to prove one of the finest Presidents the RHS ever had. His first recorded visit to Nymans was in 1927 and thereafter his name occurs often in the visitors' book. He was a good friend of the Messels and undoubtedly his championship of their garden was the chief reason for its ultimate survival.

During the 1920s the Far East continued to yield more treasures every year. George Forrest went on exploring western China; he was there for most of the war period and made three more expeditions between 1921 and his death in 1932. Besides introducing many new rhododendrons, Forrest is perhaps best remembered for *Primula malacoides* and *Gentiana sino-ornata*. In 1924 he sent seed of *Camellia saluenensis* to J. C. Williams: when this came into flower at Caerhays it was crossed with *C. japonica* to produce a new race of hardy hybrids, *C.* × *williamsii*. This is J. Williams's greatest claim to immortality, and many varieties of this beautiful shrub now transform our gardens in early spring.

Caerhays, Nymans, Bodnant, Borde Hill and several other gardens subscribed in some measure to Forrest's journeys in China after the war, and also to those of Frank Kingdon-Ward and the American collector, Joseph Rock. In all, Forrest made seven journeys (each of which lasted about two years) and collected 31,015 batches of seed: 5,375 of these were rhododendrons. Kingdon Ward's career as explorer and plant-hunter was not quite as dramatic and prolific as Forrest's but it lasted longer; he made twenty botanical or geographical expeditions in the forty-seven years between his first trip in 1911 and his death in 1958. Among his 23,068 packets of seed were a hundred new species of rhododendron. How many of these discoveries found a home at Nymans is uncertain, but there was plenty of room in the new piece of ground on the other side of the road (Anne's gift to her father) for a vast number to be planted out. Lennie made a particular point of keeping everything that could be persuaded to germinate, regardless of quality, a trait that was to prove invaluable for later students of the Chinese flora.

The collector whose exploits were followed with most interest at Nymans was Harold Comber. James Comber and his wife Ethel had raised three children in the gardener's cottage and the eldest, Harold, born on 31 December 1897, showed a great interest in gardening and botany from an early age, winning prizes at Cuckfield and Handcross Shows for collections of wild flowers. His parents were determined that the boy should have a good education and at twelve years old young Harold was sent to a private school, Ardingly College. (Half the fees were paid by Annie Messel and half came from his father's journalistic efforts: James Comber wrote short articles of the 'In your garden this week' type for several of the smaller gardening magazines.) Harold left Ardingly when he was fourteen and worked at Nymans for a while. His father took him round to see Leonardslee and other gardens nearby and early in 1914 he was recommended by Sir Edmund Loder to his friend Henry Elwes, of Colesbourne Park. Elwes was very kind and encouraging to the young employee, lending books on travel and plant history from his extensive library. When most of the garden staff were called up for war service Harold (then aged seventeen) was put in charge of the glasshouses and botanical collections, responsibilities not usually given to anyone so young. When he in turn became eligible for the army he was pronounced unfit due to a knee injury and was sent to a munitions factory for the duration of the war.

In 1918 Harold Comber went to work at Bletchingly Castle, Surrey, and then, in 1920, was sponsored by Sir Edmund Loder and Henry Elwes to follow a course of study at the Botanic Gardens, Edinburgh. Here he passed competitive examinations in twenty-one subjects with an average mark of 85 per cent. Although he was happy working for a time in the glasshouses there, he always nurtured a desire to go plant-hunting. He had hopes of accompanying Forrest to China on one expedition, but was disappointed. In 1925 his chance came when he was asked to lead an expedition to South America. Little systematic collecting had been done in that part of the world since the time of William Lobb, and a syndicate of gardeners, headed by Henry McLaren of Bodnant, planned to remedy this. The special aim of the venture was to collect not only new plants (or those which were only known from herbarium specimens) but to search for the hardiest possible forms of plants which were already in cultivation. Naturally the Messels wished to subscribe to the syndicate and Nymans was to benefit enormously from young Comber's work.

Harold Comber spent two summers in South America (1925/6 and

Harold Comber *c.* 1930

1926/7) collecting, working mostly in the Andean provinces of Neuquen in Argentina and Valdivia in Chile, where climatic conditions were considered similar to those in Britain. Not only his sponsors but his parents, too, were delighted when he returned to England in 1927 with quantities of seed. The fine South American plants already growing at Nymans were mostly in their prime and it was a fascinating task to compare the new material with the old. *Eucryphia lucida* var. *milliganii* was new to the garden but *E. cordifolia*, collected at high altitude, did not prove any hardier than the existing trees. New forms of *Embothrium coccineum* and *Desfontainia spinosa* did well and *Nothofagus obliqua* found conditions greatly to its liking, growing fast and soon producing seedlings. There was already a good collection of berberis at Nymans and several more were added, including *B.* × *lologensis* and *B. linearifolia*, both of which were to prove excellent garden plants. Although many of the Andean trees and shrubs adapted well to the climate of the British Isles, a number of eminently desirable herbaceous and alpine species proved either impossible to cultivate or soon died out. More than twenty discoveries bear Harold Comber's name (including a new genus, *Combera*), but unfortunately few of these will grow away from their homeland.

The very attractive but difficult mutisias, *M. decurrens, M. oligodon* and *M. retusa*, all natives of South America, had been known for some time, but Harold Comber brought back fresh seed for his father to nurture. These grew and flowered magnificently at Nymans and James Comber wrote an article on their cultivation for the RHS *Journal*. Like so many other exotic species they did not survive his demise, and are seldom seen today in other than very sheltered gardens. *Triptilion spinosum*, a blue composite planted round the croquet lawn, was the pride of Nymans for many years. It died out completely and is apparently unobtainable today, awaiting reintroduction from the wild. *Asteranthera ovata*, which made a fine display at the foot of a north wall, has recently been coaxed from near extinction back to flowering size.

A large number of the Comber introductions eventually found their way to the RHS shows. Bodnant, Kew, Wakehurst and Edinburgh all brought plant material to Vincent Square: an especially good form of *Embothrium lanceolatum* raised at Bodnant was named 'Norquinco Valley' and gained a First Class Certificate in 1948. (This is the type most often seen in gardens today.) Nymans was especially proud of its plants grown from Harold Comber's seed and exhibited a great number over the years; not all won plaudits but *Calceolaria benthamii, Lathyrus magellanicus* and *Pernettya leucocarpa* received Awards of Merit in 1929, as did *Fuchsia macrostemma* in 1930. A vintage year followed in 1931 with *Berberis linearifolia* gaining a First Class Certificate, *Azara lanceolata, Berberis × lologensis* and *Solanum valdiviense* all receiving AMs, and a Lindley Medal being awarded to a group of *Triptilion spinosum*. The plant which Harold Comber himself considered his best find was *Alstroemeria ligtu angustifolia* 'Vivid' which was shown from Nymans in 1937. It gained an Award of Merit then but its true worth was discovered in later breeding programmes when its bright colour was passed on to the hybrid alstroemerias now so popular in the florists' trade.

In 1929 Comber went on another two-year collecting trip, this time to Tasmania, on behalf of a syndicate formed by Lionel de Rothschild. The climate of lowland Tasmania is mild, but many hardy variants of well known Australian plants can be found in the chilly mountain regions. In Comber's time the heart of the island was almost inaccessible: explorers had to carry their own supplies and go on foot, as there was no food available for men or horses. Consequently a fortnight was the limit of any trip and only a few plant-hunters had worked there. Comber had more success than most and was able to distribute a good amount of seed on his return to England. At Nymans part of the land on the other side of the road – that not already filled with the fruits of earlier expeditions – was devoted to his plants, but shortage of manpower during the war led to their neglect and subsequent loss. Other gardens suffered in the same way, so not much material from this expedition had time to demonstrate its virtues. Recently many Australian and New Zealand plants have been reintroduced by specialist nurseries; several of these are becoming popular garden plants although to many eyes the antipodean flora sits less comfortably in the English landscape than the rich mix available from other parts of the world. At Nymans a special effort is now being made to grow a comprehensive selection of Harold Comber's plants, both Andean and Tasmanian. The occasional connections between the two are of particular interest to botanists: *eucryphia, sophora, lomata* and *nothofagus* are among a handful of plant families which are found in both the antipodes and South America but not elsewhere around the globe.

After his return from Tasmania Harold Comber worked in the herbaria at Kew and Edinburgh for a time. He gave a lecture to the RHS in July 1931 about his Tasmanian expedition, but unlike some of the other great plant-hunters he did not write any books about his travels. From 1933 to 1946 he was at the Burnham Lily Nursery and in 1949 he published an important new classification of the genus *lilium*.

He moved to America in 1952 where he became lily manager for Jan de Graff's Oregan Bulb Farm. Here he carried out a very successful breeding programme (the splendid lilies 'Pink Perfection', 'Green Magic' and 'Imperial Crimson' are all of his raising) and worked on *alstroemeria* also. When he retired his time was devoted to the native flora of Oregon and he compiled plant lists for the Nature Conservancy. He died in 1969.

Although Harold Comber's finds were small in number compared to those of the great Asiatic plant-hunters, the proportion of his plants which ultimately proved garden-worthy is as high as theirs. The ability to spot a good garden plant in the wild is not easily attained: Harold Comber had it in large measure and can therefore be rated as one of the great collectors of the twentieth century. When his skill as a breeder is also taken into account, his contribution to our gardens is immense.

In 1930 the RHS instituted a new award, to be conferred on persons who had rendered distinguished service to horticulture while employed in gardens or nurseries. The first thirty 'Associates of Honour' were elected that year and presented with their diplomas and badges at the Chelsea Show. Among them was James Comber, who had served his chosen profession well. It was fifty-one years since he had begun work as a garden boy and thirty-five since he had been made Head Gardener at Nymans, where he had raised the garden to the position of distinction which it now held. A member of the Rhododendron Committee, the Lily Committee and the Floral Committee of the RHS, as well as a regular contributor to the *Gardeners' Chronicle* and other journals, frequently a judge at flower shows, both around the country and at Vincent Square, Comber had been tireless in promoting everything that was best in gardening. It was a proud day for all at Nymans when he received this public recognition of his skill and dedication.

Comber was now reaching retirement age, so his foreman, Cecil Nice, who had worked at Nymans since 1924, was designated to succeed him as Head Gardener. But Comber was still full of vigour and had no intention of relinquishing control, nor did Lennie really want him to. As a result his retirement was in name only and Cecil Nice was obliged to operate in the shadow of the older man's forceful personality for many years to come.

Nymans was the subject of a long article in *Country Life* in September 1932, signed by G. C. Taylor, their gardening editor. A fine set of black-and-white photographs illustrated the article and Taylor wrote in glowing terms: 'It is seldom that one meets with a garden where the

This is to Certify that

James Comber

in recognition of his services
to Horticulture was elected an

Associate of Honour
of the
Royal Horticultural Society

On the ___23rd___ day of ___April___ 1930

Witness _our hands and Seal at Westminster_

this ___6th___ day of ___May___ 1930

_____ PRESIDENT.

_____ SECRETARY.

James Comber's Associate of Honour certificate

virtues of those two great classes of gardeners which, for want of better names, are best described as the plant collectors and the picture makers, are so happily married as they are at Nymans. It is this dual quality that at once stamps Nymans, even to the most casual observer, as a garden of distinction, the product and expression of those who are not only lovers of fine and choice plants but lovers of good and picturesque gardening . . .' After giving the history of the garden and discoursing on the 'amazing wealth' of plants it contained; Taylor continued: 'Nymans is a garden as full of achievement as it is of promise, displaying in the remarkable scope and variety of its plant furnishings a catholic taste, originality and vision, combined with skilful cultivation. It reveals the success that comes from intelligent experiment, that adds so much to the interest and zeal of gardening and has contributed so handsomely to our store of plant knowledge.'

For several years Lennie had been building up yet another specialist collection, this time of early botanical treatises and ancient herbals. It may have been Maud's interest in scented plants which had first aroused his enthusiasm (was Redouté's *Les Roses*, one of his early purchases, a present for his wife perhaps?) but by the end of the 1920s Nymans was known to have one of the best horticultural libraries in the world, only surpassed in England by those of the British Museum and the Royal Horticultural Society. In 1933 Eleanor Sinclair Rohde, a writer with a particular interest in garden history, published an article on the Messel collection in the RHS *Journal*. Miss Rohde lived at Cranham Lodge, Surrey; she was a friend of Gertrude Jekyll and Vita Sackville-West and also knew Lennie's brother-in-law, Eric Parker, collaborating with him on *The Gardener's Week-end Book*. Between 1920 and 1924 she had written three books on gardening, with special emphasis on the use of herbs, and her first recorded visit to Nymans was in 1929. *The Scented Garden*, published in 1931, has the dedication: 'To Maud Messel, with thanks to Colonel Messel and Mr J.Comber'. Some of the photographs for the book were taken by Oliver. Eleanor Sinclair Rohde's later books also contain several references to Nymans and the many kindnesses she received there.

Miss Rohde's article in the RHS *Journal* does not give a complete list of all the books in the Nymans library but she describes the most notable items, adding comments about their authors and their influence on contemporary thought. The earliest volume in Lennie's possession was printed about 1480 and he had at least ten other important herbals which pre-dated 1520. All were written in Latin, Europe's common language at that time, and many were still in their original tooled leather bindings. In addition there were fourteen books written in German, thirteen in Flemish, seventeen in Italian and twenty-eight in French, as well as eight Swiss publications, many of them beautifully illustrated and very rare. The collection of English herbals was particularly fine, including nearly all notable works published between the sixteenth and nineteenth centuries. Tragically, the whole of this priceless collection was to be destroyed by fire only a few years after the article was published.

Rhododendron keysii

Chapter Eight

Family Affairs

By the early 1930s Maud and Lennie were seriously worried about Anne's marriage. Ronald was very ambitious; his work kept him busy and he soon grew tired of the endless round of parties, the dressing up and all the theatrical gossip which his wife enjoyed so much. Anne determined to do as she pleased and the couple ceased to go everywhere together. In 1933 they agreed to have a trial separation.

Foremost among Anne's escorts and admirers was a very eligible young man, possessed of an ancient Irish title and a fine estate at Birr, Co. Offaly, seventy miles west of Dublin: Michael Parsons, 6th Earl of Rosse. A contemporary of Oliver's at Eton, he had known the Messel family since his teens. He had been too young for any romantic attachment when Anne was in her twenties but by the time she was thirty and seeking escape from an unhappy marriage the age gap hardly mattered. Anne's first visit to Birr set the seal on what was to prove a passionate and enduring love affair.

The estate at Birr had descended from father to son in direct line for ten generations. Laurence Parsons had arrived in Ireland in about 1590 and was knighted for his services to the English crown in 1612. In 1620 he acquired over one thousand acres of land: this included the town of Birr and a castle which he greatly enlarged, although most of his work was burnt in the Rebellion of 1643. His grandson, another Laurence, was created a baronet in 1677 and rebuilt the property, adding a very handsome staircase of yew which still survives. Two generations later the 3rd baronet (who became 2nd Earl of Rosse when an uncle died in 1807) altered the castle and outbuildings again, this time in the Gothick taste. Much of his work was intact, although awaiting the hand of the restorer, when Anne first went to Birr. But it was Michael's great-grandfather, William, 3rd Earl of Rosse, who had really put the place on the map. One of the most distinguished and inventive astronomers of his time, William Rosse designed and built the largest telescope in

Birr Castle, Ireland. The north front

the world. Ready for use in 1841 and not superseded until 1917, it offered an unparalleled view of the heavens to any astronomer prepared to venture into this remote corner of Ireland.

Michael was only twelve years old when his father died of wounds received in the Great War. Although his mother ran the estate during his minority the young heir developed an abiding interest in the grounds surrounding the castle, which had been landscaped in the latter part of the eighteenth century. The lake, the clumps of fine old trees and winding walks, made a charming setting for the little Gothick castle, perched on a crag above the rushing waters of the river Camcor. As the 5th Earl had been a subscriber to two of Wilson's expeditions to China there were many young trees in the park and Michael soon became an expert dendrologist. During his lifetime he steadily increased the collection at Birr until it became one of the best in the country.

Michael's enthusiasm for his trees was matched by Anne's knowledge of gardening, while his other great interest, the preservation of the Georgian buildings at Birr, thrilled her too. (Even a non-scientist could not fail to be impressed by the mysterious brooding bulk of the great telescope which dominated the view across the park.) So much could be done together in this enchanted place that it was easy to cast the brittle London life aside. Divorce, although troublesome and degrading, no longer meant social ostracism – other members of their circle were changing partners and Ronald did not apparently raise many objections. The children were very young and in an amicable settlement they surely would not suffer.

Lennie and Maud, raised in the firm belief that marriage was for ever, must have been saddened by the breach. The family had all liked Ronald and many in the Messel circle found Anne's behaviour reprehensible. The Armstrong-Jones's divorce was declared absolute on 28 August 1935: three weeks later Anne and Michael were married. It was a quiet affair this time with only close friends and family present. However, the Messels were soon reconciled to the new arrangement; Michael's intelligence and sympathy, his wide-ranging interests and his skilful handling of the wilful Anne quickly won their affection and respect. Ronald also re-married, so everyone was happy – except perhaps the children: even well-disposed step parents and loving grandparents are no compensation for a fragmented upbringing.

The Earl and Countess of Rosse at Birr Castle by Oliver Messel

In the first four years after their wedding the Earl and Countess of Rosse were very busy putting Birr to rights. Anne transformed the interior of the castle: already an expert in early eighteenth-century furniture she knew exactly what should be done to make the rooms look their best. The garden too was born again. From their earliest years both Anne and Michael had been accustomed to watch over the growth of young plants from the Sino-Himalayas and they were eager to obtain yet more rarities from the fabled lands of the great plant-hunters. Their honeymoon was spent in China and while there they set in motion plans for a new series of expeditions, which in due course enriched the gardens of the West still further.

Maud and Lennie visited their daughter's new home many times and were enraptured by its beauty. The link between Nymans and Birr was to be of great advantage to both gardens. Improvements were carried out, plants propagated and exchanged, and many happy hours were spent discussing horticultural subjects. The Messels had always taken a spring holiday abroad each year, as well as making regular visits to Scotland and Ireland for the salmon fishing, Lennie's favourite sport. Now the Rosses joined them on holiday and all four went botanising together. In Maud's letters to Michael (spread over many years) she thanks him for his kindness on these happy excursions and also for his gifts of books, plants and seeds: she describes how well the cuttings he had given her are growing and what fine gardens she has recently visited and enjoyed. James Comber was invited to visit Birr also, and found much to admire there: the estate had one priceless asset lacking at Nymans – plenty of water. The lake, the river which ran through the park, and the rain (not too much, as Birr is in the centre of Ireland) must have made him envious.

The Messels' pride and delight knew no bounds when it became clear that Anne had inherited her grandfather's genius for design and for dramatic effects: it was she who was primarily responsible for the new gardens which were taking shape at Birr. On the sunny terraces between the castle and the river a rich mixture of old-fashioned favourites overhung the paths, scenting the air. Near the lake ancient forest trees of giant proportions were interplanted with magnolias, viburnums and other early-flowering shrubs; here secret shady corners and sudden glimpses of fresh delights lured the walker onwards, just as they did at Nymans. *Eucryphia* 'Nymansay', the rhododendrons raised by James Comber, Andean and Tasmanian discoveries brought back by Harold Comber, all found a home to their liking, as did the great drifts of 'Blue-eyed Mary' beneath the trees, another echo of Nymans.

Away from the river, on the other side of the park, lay the kitchen garden, the orchards and the old formal garden with its ancient box hedges, the tallest in the world. This area had suffered from neglect so there was opportunity for Anne to rescue and replant as well as to devise a completely new garden, this time quite unlike anything at Nymans. Based on a seventeenth-century design, gravel walks and clipped box surrounded beds of lilac and roses, with urns and statues marking focal points in a strictly formal layout. The tall encircling hornbeam hedges, trained over arches and with windows cut to look inwards only, make a delightful green cloister walk, ideal for contemplation. Anne's drawings and notes for the planting schemes have been preserved, as has her sketch for the wooden seat design with its crossed Rs which stands at the head of the main axis path.

Michael was devoted to his parents-in-law and their garden. In 1971, long after Maud and Lennie were dead, he gave a lecture on Nymans to the RHS. Of Lennie he said, 'His knowledge of horticultural matters was quite exceptional. He genuinely loved his plants and they gave him real excitement. . . furthermore he had an unusual ability to impart his own enthusiasm to others. I learned an immense amount from him and indeed nobody could spend even a few moments with him in any garden without gaining some new information.' On Maud: 'Her feeling for plants was essentially sentimental and each favourite had for her its very own personality . . . she had a magic touch with propagation, as if she were able to impart to plants the properties of a fairy wand of love.'

Nymans was at its zenith during the 1930s. Ludwig's early plantings were now mature, new material was still flowing in, and regular successes at Vincent Square kept the garden in the public eye. At the Conifer Conference and Exhibition in the autumn of 1931 a magnificent collection of growing trees and cone-bearing branches, from gardens all over the British Isles, was on show. Among the fifty or so exhibitors were all the leading nurserymen of the day as well as many private gardens, with Bodnant, Wakehurst Place, Borde Hill and Nymans making particularly good displays. *Conifers in Cultivation*, the report on the conference published the following year, gave lists of trees, with their age and size, compiled from information sent in by two hundred and fifty owners. Some of the trees at Nymans had reached record size: an *Abies veitchii* at 81 feet 3 inches was believed to be the tallest of its kind in the British Isles and a *Cedrus atlantica* at 105 feet the second tallest. Examples of *Picea omorika* and *Pinus pinaster* were also very fine.

In the period from 1928 to 1938 various rhododendron species from Nymans, grown from collectors' seed, won seven Awards of Merit and two First Class Certificates at the RHS shows. But it was not only rhododendrons which occupied a special place in the hearts of Lennie and his head gardener: many other shrubs, trees, climbers and bulbs, some hardy, some grown under glass, went to the show bench. A display of *Lilium duchartrei* var. *farreri* won a Silver Medal in 1925 and one of *L. d.* var. *wardii* gained a First Class Certificate in 1930; *Forsythia atrocaulis* 'Nymans variety' was given an AM in 1934. In 1935 and 1936 Nymans won medals for exhibits of terrestrial orchids. These had been collected by Maud and Lennie on their holidays in southern Europe and installed in the old greenhouses in the Top Garden on their return, where they flourished exceedingly. When shown at Vincent Square they aroused so much public interest that Comber wrote an article for the RHS *Journal* entitled 'The cultivation of Terrestrial Orchids in pots'. Of course not all exhibits won prizes: the great benefit of the system was that garden lovers attending the shows were able to see a

Leonard Messel and his daughter, Anne, in an Irish nursery garden

wide range of plants which were either particularly well grown, exceptionally rare, or of special botanical interest.

Lennie was elected to serve on the RHS Council in 1936 and the following year James Comber received another accolade, the Victoria Medal of Honour in Horticulture. This is the highest honour the Society can bestow. It had been instituted in 1897 as part of the celebrations for Queen Victoria's Diamond Jubilee and the recipients were at first limited to sixty, one for each year of the Queen's reign, but on her death in 1901 this number was raised to sixty three. Only when a medal holder dies is another elected, so that the total remains constant. Among the famous gardeners who had already been given the honour were many who knew Nymans well and had influenced its development: W. Jackson Bean, Joseph Cheal, Henry Elwes, George Forrest, John Heal, Gertrude Jekyll, Frank Kingdon-Ward, Irwin Lynch, Johnny Millais, Lionel de Rothschild, Harry Veitch, Lord Wakehurst, P. D. Williams, Ellen Willmott and Ernest Wilson. Comber received his medal from the hands of Lord Aberconway on 9 February 1937. Another great Sussex gardener, Stephenson R. Clarke of Borde Hill, was awarded the VMH on the same day.

Maud's love of plants, especially roses, was well known. It was her habit to beg cuttings from any friend she visited, not just from their garden but from drawing-room vase or bridal bouquet. Many rarities arrived at Nymans in this way, old gardens in Scotland or the south of France being the best hunting grounds. Fellow rose-enthusiasts such as Ellen Willmott and E. A. Bunyard came to admire Maud's collection and great was her delight when it was confirmed that a rose which had grown on the gardener's cottage since pre-Messel days was 'Blush Noisette', believed extinct and known only from an illustration in Redouté's *Les Roses*. Another pilgrim to Nymans in the 1930s was Graham Stuart Thomas, then a young man working for a Surrey nursery. He came to admire and to gather knowledge, later distilled in several important books on old-fashioned roses which helped to bring these neglected beauties back into favour.

Lennie became High Sheriff of Sussex in 1936. He and Maud were very active in local affairs and did much good work in the nearby villages of Handcross, Slaugham and Staplefield. A member of the Parochial Church Council since 1919, Lennie presented Staplefield Church with several valuable fittings, including the east window and the oak screen for the chapel that was dedicated to Muriel's memory. Maud took a personal interest in the Women's Institute, the Mother's Union, the British Legion and the Red Cross, but she was especially loved for her enthusiastic support of the local Shakespeare Society. Costumes for their productions were lent from her own wardrobe, or else designed and made by herself, and performances took place at Nymans where the Great Hall and minstrels' gallery made a perfect setting. The garden was opened for fêtes and charitable events, and a May Day pageant, first organised by Maud in 1919 as a tonic against post-war gloom, became a regular highlight of the local calendar. Everyone dressed up and went in procession round Staplefield Green, a May Queen was crowned and there was country dancing and feasting at Nymans afterwards.

The Messels did not open their garden solely for local benefit. When Queen Alexandra died in 1926 a fund was set up in her memory to help finance the District Nursing Service. Various ideas were put forward by the organisers as to how best to raise money: one suggestion was that people with fine gardens – not necessarily large or grand ones – might like to open them to visitors on one day a year. The gate money was to be kept low and all would be welcome. The response exceeded all expectations and in 1927 six hundred private gardens opened in aid of the charity. Over £8,000 was raised and so much enthusiasm generated that it was decided to continue the National Gardens Scheme, as it became known, on an annual basis. A network of County organisers was established and by 1932 nearly a thousand gardens in England and Wales were open to the public on different days, from spring right through to autumn.

To owners and their staff the challenge of getting everything to look its best on a certain day was enormously stimulating. At Nymans Lennie and Comber, growing old together, had become resistant to change and hardly noticed how overcrowded their beloved garden had become. Pruning was always low on the list of their priorities: paths were narrowed by bulging shrubs, climbers wreathed every over-hanging branch and great masses of rhododendrons made impenetrable thickets. The sheltering trees had grown too tall and distant views, once the glory of Nymans, were half obscured. The prospect of more public visiting meant that a fresh look was taken at some of these faults.

At first 'open days' at Nymans were held only in the spring, but it was soon decided to extend the season as the many varieties of eucryphia, flowering mainly in July and August, were a treat worth coming miles to see. Hydrangeas too did well here, their usual pinks and reds changing to splendid shades of blue and purple in the light loamy soil. The best colour came from varieties of *Hydrangea opuloides*, and Lennie arranged for many more to be planted

A visitors' day at Nymans, July 1939. The Sunk Garden and Italian loggia

throughout the garden. *H. villosa* (one of Wilson's intoductions), *H. sargentiana*, *H. paniculata* and the climbing *H. petiolaris* all added their special contribution, making a feast for the eye in late summer. Some thinning and felling took place in the Pinetum and *Eucryphia* 'Nymansay' was used to fill the gaps, its chalk-white blossom most effective against the sombre greens and golds of the conifers. In front, blocks of hydrangeas and clumps of pampas grass transformed this end of the garden, keeping it colourful until the autumn – a bold and imaginative piece of planting worthy of Ludwig himself.

The Messels continued to play host to specialist garden-lovers. In 1935 a group of Swedish dendrologists on a tour of southern England came to Nymans; it was, they declared, the highlight of their trip. They were followed (in 1937) by the Crown Prince of Sweden, who went so far as to bring his own gardener with him to take notes. But for the Messels the late 1930s were a time of winding down. The London house was used less and less; Nymans, secluded within its girdle of trees, became more than ever a retreat from the pressures and perplexities of modern life.

Lennie was sixty-five in 1937. Although he never ceased to be senior partner at L. Messel & Co. and continued to draw most of his income from the firm, his interest in its affairs dwindled. Linley Messel never showed much aptitude for the work but among the younger partners was Ruth and Eric Parker's eldest son (also called Eric), who had a very good head for business. His efforts led to a resurgence in the firm's fortunes and this – coupled with shrewd and kindly advice to friends and relatives – enabled several members of the now extended Messel family to continue in the style of living to which they were accustomed.

Although Maud and Lennie were well-cushioned against stress and financial hardship they could not avoid noticing how much the world outside their private paradise was changing. In Europe Hitler's persecution of the Jews and the prospect of another war brought great anxiety, although by this time the family's Englishness was not in doubt. Lennie's only remaining link with Germany was with the daughter of his uncle, Alfred Messel. Irene was considerably younger than her English cousin and at first was not at risk, being protected by her father's famous name. Alfred Messel's work was much admired by the young architects who were hammering out the 'modern' style during the 1920s and 1930s. But when Hitler intensified his efforts to rid Germany of anyone with even a dash of Jewish blood she and her husband were in grave danger of being deported to a concentration camp. Lennie sent money and pulled strings to enable them to escape and later gave generous support in their struggle to build a new life.

In England the great estates were breaking up. Death duties had risen from 8 per cent in 1904 to 50 per cent in 1930, agricultural rents had fallen throughout the period and landowners found themselves in increasing difficulties, obliged to pull down their crumbling mansions and sell off heirlooms in order to survive. The old guard could only deplore these reversals of fortune but among the younger generation one or two voices began to be raised in protest: surely a few remnants of England's great and glorious cultural heritage could be saved for posterity to enjoy. Some rescue organisation (either private or public) must be set up.

The National Trust, launched in 1895 'to preserve places of historic interest or natural beauty', was among the first to respond to this appeal. In its early days the Trust had devoted most of its energy to protecting the natural environment. Parts of the Lake District, the Peak District of Derbyshire and several stretches of coastline had been saved from development, and many important archaeological sites preserved. A few houses were also acquired, more by chance than design; these were small masterpieces of the medieval and Tudor periods, such as the medieval priest's house at Alfriston, and from the 1930s the Trust also began to take on the homes of famous personages. Barrington Court in Somerset was the first large house to come to the Trust (in 1907), but after that there was a long gap before the great Elizabethan pile of Montacute, also in Somerset, was given in 1931.

During the 1930s the ideas which motivated the Trust's work gradually gained credence and membership numbers, which had been tiny at first, slowly rose: in 1928 there had been 1,550 members, in 1933 there were 2,750. By then it was clear that prompt and vigorous action would be needed if some of the finest buildings in the country were to be saved from ruin. Various proposals were put forward at the National Trust's AGM in 1934 and the discussion which followed led to the formation of the Trust's Historic Country Houses Committee, charged with discovering what sort of rescue scheme might appeal to those owners whose properties were most at risk.

It was not only the impoverished country estates which were in need of championship: the towns, London especially, were being torn down and rebuilt at a great rate. Georgian buildings were not sancrosanct and many fell to the developer: Devonshire House, by William Kent, came down in 1930; Rennie's Waterloo Bridge and the Adam brothers' Adelphi were demolished in 1936; Nash's Regent Street was rebuilt, his Carlton House Terrace threatened. The unity of Portman Square, Cavendish Square and Portland Place was destroyed by new building, and many hundreds of lesser streets and squares were redeveloped. Michael, Anne and Oliver were all passionate devotees of the eighteenth century, and together with a few kindred souls they appealed for a stand to be made against the destruction of Georgian London. The National Trust had primarily concerned itself with buildings in landscape rather than urban architecture and the Society for the Preservation of Ancient Buildings (founded by William Morris in 1878 with the original intention of protecting medieval churches from insensitive alteration) had no interest in the fate of anything built after 1700, nor was there any other body devoted to the cause of conservation. After intense lobbying, the SPAB agreed to countenance an offshoot which would deal with the hitherto despised eighteenth century. Thus, in April 1937, the Georgian Group came into being.

Unlike the rather staid members of the SPAB, the Georgian Group was essentially a young social set, determined to enjoy themselves. By 1939 they could boast thirty-three peers of the realm among their number. Michael and Anne were leading spirits from the first and early fund-raising events were essentially light-hearted: a Georgian Ball (with decorations by Oliver) was followed by a *fête champêtre* at Osterley Park. German bombs were soon to destroy more of London than the developers had, but the seeds of a worldwide movement for the preservation of historic cities had been sown.

Meanwhile the National Trust was making headway with its Country Houses Scheme. It was clear that nothing could be done without support from the Government and after much negotiation the National Trust Act of 1937 (which exempted a house bequeathed to the Trust from death duties, and any endowment from income tax) was passed, followed by another Act in 1939 which tied up some loose ends. The Trust also declared that they would always carry out the wishes of the testators and make arrangements for the family of the previous owner to continue living in the house. With such positive encouragement things got off to a good start, and in spite of the intervention of the war Wightwick Manor, Blickling Hall, West Wycombe Park, Cliveden, Polesden Lacey and Lacock Abbey all came to the Trust under varying forms of agreement between 1937 and 1943. Much of the National Trust's success in this field was due to James Lees-Milne. A founder-member of the Georgian Group and close friend of Michael and Anne, he had begun working for the Trust in 1936. Called up at the begining of the war, he was invalided out of the army after two years and went back to the Trust at the end of 1941.

Michael joined the Irish Guards in 1939 and later served in the Normandy campaign with the Guards' Armoured Division. His championship of eighteenth-century architecture had already marked him out as a potential leader of the National Trust and his first appointment was to the Country House Committee in 1943. In the cities huge bomb-damage clearance schemes were undertaken immediately after the war. The local authorities made no effort to save the smaller Georgian terraces, many of which could easily have been repaired. Michael was elected chairman of the Georgian Group in 1946 and it was his energetic leadership which did so much to turn the tide of popular opinion against this unnecessary destruction.

Throughout the Second World War normal life was suspended. Gardeners and nurserymen were particularly hard hit: no fuel allowance was given for hothouses, and from 1943 onwards it was forbidden to send any horticultural material by post or rail. Ground used for hardy plants and shrubs went under the plough and in many cases an entire nursery stock, the work of generations of growers, was lost. The great collections of ornamental trees and shrubs up and down the land had to fend for themselves, but they naturally suffered less than the more labour-intensive type of garden. The RHS did its best to keep interest in horticulture alive, managing in spite of the general shortage of paper to produce their *Journal* all through the war. Some of the older members were asked to contribute articles, and in 1940 a series appeared called 'Features of my Garden'. These were well-known gardens described by their owners: Bodnant by Lord Aberconway, Abbotswood by Mark Fenwick, Exbury by Lionel de Rothschild, and Nymans by Leonard Messel.

At Nymans only three elderly men – Comber was seventy-three in 1939 – were left to run the garden, out of a staff of at least eleven. Two Land Army girls were drafted in to help on the estate, but severe cut-backs were inevitable. Although flower gardening was not encouraged by the Government, great emphasis was laid on the cultivation of essential food supplies. Householders were urged to keep chickens, and if possible pigs, to augment the meagre rations; even the smallest plot of land could be used for vegetables, and the RHS performed a valuable service in giving advice to amateur growers.

Although the big annual show at Chelsea was cancelled for the duration, small shows at Vincent Square continued on an irregular basis. None was held during the winter of 1939/40, nor during the worst months of the blitz in 1941. They began again in 1942 but were forbidden altogether by Government decree in 1943. Nymans sent in a few exhibits during this period, but it was left to Borde Hill to introduce what was to prove one of the most popular and successful flowering shrubs of recent years – *Camellia* 'Donation' – which received an Award of Merit in 1941.

By the beginning of 1945 it was clear that the war could not last much longer and the RHS, still under the presidency of Lord Aberconway, began to make plans for a more hopeful future. Shows were resumed, but the subscription had to be raised for the first time in fifty years – from one guinea to two. Lennie, who had served on the Council from 1936 until 1941, was presented with the Victoria Medal of Honour for his work as a keen amateur gardener and grower of rare plants. At the Society's AGM in 1946 Lord Aberconway said, 'Colonel Messel's father set out to grow in his wonderful garden at Nymans every hardy tree and shrub that could be grown out of doors in this country, and he succeeded in a very great number of doubtful cases. His son for more than thirty years has kept up that high standard and you can see no more interesting garden than Colonel Messel's.'

Chapter Nine

The Garden in Jeopardy

T he Messel family suffered more bereavement in the Second World War than they had in the First, with two of Ruth's boys and one of Hilda's killed in action. Lennie's eldest son Linley served in the Middle East with the Middlesex Yeomanry, rising to the rank of Lieutenant-Colonel. He had married Anne Alexander in 1933, but before returning home at the end of the campaign made up his mind that he wanted a divorce. He refused to discuss the matter with his parents, corresponded with his wife only through a third party, and took no interest in his children's future. Maud and Lennie were very hurt by this attitude and felt that their daughter-in-law had been cruelly wronged. Nor were they able to establish cordial relations with their son's second wife, whom he married in 1945. Unlike Anne's divorce and remarriage, Linley's affairs held no silver lining for his parents; to their sorrow the rift between them was never fully healed.

Oliver Messel was a captain in the Camouflage Unit of the Royal Engineers during the war, stationed at Norwich. He was several times granted short spells of leave to work in the theatre (considered essential for keeping up the morale of civilians as well as troops) and was finally released from the army in 1944 to design Gabriel Pascal's film *Caesar and Cleopatra*. This is probably the most enduring monument to Oliver's skills, but his work for the ballet has gone down in history too. In February 1946 the Opera House at Covent Garden was reopened with a production of *The Sleeping Beauty* for which Oliver designed the sets and costumes. This was a resounding success, both in England and later when the production went to America. Oliver's genius for improvisation was invaluable at this time, and he worked wonders in spite of the acute shortage of raw materials.

Oliver Messel, 1942

By this time Maud and Lennie had six grandchildren. Four of them – Linley's two daughters, Elizabeth and Victoria, and the Rosses' two sons, William and Martin – were born between 1934 and 1939. (Martin was the only member of the family to be born at Nymans, an occasion for great rejoicing on the estate.) Close ties of affection had already been established with Anne's children by her first marriage. Although Susan and Tony Armstrong-Jones shared holiday times equally between their mother and father, it was the Messel grandparents who provided the most stable feature of their lives. The six children spent many happy times together at Nymans as well as at Birr and Womersley, the Rosse property in Yorkshire. The Messel clan had extended greatly: they all kept in touch even though it was not easy during the war and its aftermath to organise such big family gatherings as had taken place in Ludwig's time.

Victoria Messel beside a Japanese
lantern in the Heath Garden, 1942

The younger generation were all assured of a warm and loving
welcome at Nymans, but it was Victoria who spent most time there.
Her mother worked in London during the war and her elder sister went
to boarding school, but Victoria and her nanny were housed in one of
the cottages on the estate. The little girl had the run of the garden,
which was rapidly becoming overgrown through lack of proper
maintenance. The dark mysterious evergreens, the winding paths and
secret hiding places never failed to enchant, and she had happy
memories too of the glasshouses, where the under-gardeners would
turn a blind eye to surreptitious sampling of peaches and grapes.
(Comber was still a towering figure to be feared and admired, just as he
had been for the previous generation.) A lasting impression of married
bliss and contented old age was left on Victoria by her grandparents.
Observing their unfailing gentle courtesy, she was especially struck
with how often they sat quietly together, not talking but just holding
hands. Maud's arthritis made walking painful and she took early to the
benefit of a wheel chair: Lennie was always solicitous of her comfort

Magnolia stellata along the North Drive, Scots pine and Norway spruce behind

and for even the briefest parting – such as his daily stroll around the garden – would kiss his wife a tender goodbye.

The long period of austerity which followed the end of the war was, for many people, even harder to bear than the multitude of deprivations they had suffered while it lasted. Practically no material was available for repairs or any kind of building work; glasshouses which had closed for lack of fuel remained unusable, food rationing was even tighter than before. Petrol, coal, gas and electricity were all restricted, as were clothes, household furnishings and travel abroad. In the big country houses, many of which had been in a parlous state for decades, army billeting and general neglect had wreaked much havoc. Fortunately Nymans had not been requisitioned, although the Messels housed evacuees, schoolmasters from the Buckingham Gate Central School, which had moved to Handcross to escape the bombs in London.

The greatest difficulty to be faced by the middle and upper classes after the war was the lack of servants. Once so plentiful, they did not return to work in private houses and the old way of life was almost insupportable without them. The Messels had always been lucky with their staff; a few faithful elderly retainers and girls from the village continued to help indoors, and all their gardeners came back to work as soon as they were demobilised. Even so, it was a struggle to retain a modicum of comfort in the big, rambling house, and much time and energy would be needed to reinstate the glory of the garden. The bitterly cold winter of 1946/7 was hard for everyone to bear: for many weeks on end a thin sprinkling of snow fell daily, every tree and bush was encased in a coat of ice, and the ground stayed iron-hard with frost. At least there were plenty of logs to burn: chopping wood was about the only task the outdoor staff at Nymans could find to do, as no garden work was possible. Inside the house frozen pipes were a great problem, and a plumber with a blow-lamp was repeatedly on call. This blow-lamp was probably the cause of the disaster which overtook Nymans and the Messels one February night in 1947.

Lennie's health had been poor for some time and early that month he underwent a minor operation. His seventy-fifth birthday fell on 19 February. At about 3 a.m. that day he woke to find his room full of smoke. Rising from his sick-bed – the first time he had got up unaided – he went round the house to wake the eight people who were sleeping there that night. No one had opportunity to snatch up more than a few personal belongings, and by the time help arrived the whole place was alight. Over seventy firemen fought the blaze but their work was greatly hampered by the bitter cold. Stand-pipes were frozen and the only available water was in a pond some way below the house. With great difficulty this was pumped up to the fire engines, but it was then found that the extending ladders were useless because their runners were frozen solid. Thus it was impossible to tackle the fire efficiently from above and water could only be directed at the walls, where it at once formed sheets of icicles. Maud and Lennie, elderly and frail, could do nothing but watch their house and all its treasures burn. Most of the villagers and estate workers did not awake to the tragedy until dawn: then it was Comber, aged eighty-one but with energy and decisiveness still unimpaired, who organised a salvage team. A few things were rescued but all the best pictures, tapestries, furniture and, saddest of all, the priceless botanical library, were totally destroyed.

Anne and Michael came post-haste from Ireland as soon as they heard the news, and other members of the family gathered round. Sympathy and affection were showered upon the Messels but the loss of Nymans was a blow from which they could hardly be expected to recover. However, they bore it with the utmost stoicism, assuring every kind enquirer that the only thing that really mattered was that no one had been killed or injured in the fire. Temporary accommodation was found nearby where they could recuperate and try to plan their future. The damage to Nymans was so extensive that repairs were deemed impracticable; any building work was difficult at the time and a new house in the same elaborate style could not possibly be contemplated. Taxes were increasing and labour costs rising: the upkeep of a large garden was another luxury that even the well-off might not be able to afford. The sensible thing to do would be to sell the whole estate and retire to some much smaller place.

A week after the fire, on 27 March 1947, Lennie made a new will. Apart from £50,000 invested in L. Messel and a few small personal bequests, his trustees were empowered to sell all his property to create a trust fund for Maud's benefit during her lifetime. After her death the three children were to take equal shares from the trust. At this time Lennie must have felt that neither he nor Nymans had any future, but when spring came after the dreadful winter hope began to stir. The garden itself was untouched by the disaster and seemed more beautiful than ever. Also there was an unexpected bonus – the roofless ruin with its empty traceried windows cast a more romantic aura over the grounds than even Maud could have imagined possible. The shrubs and climbers on the walls, deeply rooted in the frozen earth, had survived the conflagration and soon softened the horror by twining through the broken stonework, flowering even more magnificently than of old. To sell the beloved place and abandon the work of two generations would be another heartbreak. For the time being at least the staff could continue to run the garden as before, while from a base nearby Maud and Lennie would visit regularly.

Fortunately the Messels were able to buy Holmsted Manor, only a few miles away from Nymans. The house was comfortable, if architecturally undistinguished, with a pleasant garden to provide a new focus of interest, and life here was constructed to be as like the old ways as possible. In spite of Lennie's indifferent health and retiring habits (he was always a rather distant figure to his grandchildren), he and Maud retained all their early enthusiasm for beautiful things and it was not long before Holmsted took on the unmistakable stamp of their taste.

At Nymans, the garden 'open days' were still kept up, and the Messels decided to undertake repairs to that part of the house which had not been irreparably damaged in the fire. Oliver provided sketches for rebuilding: the main approach was now to be through the service courtyard, with the façade of the old north wing transformed into one of his charming Gothick fantasies. But the long-term future of the property was still in doubt: neither Linley nor Oliver had ever shown

James Comber and Leonard Messel,
1947

much interest in the upkeep or development of the garden, and were unlikely to do so after their parents' death. This left Anne as the natural heiress, but as Michael's wife she was already mistress of two large estates, Birr and Womersley; to administer a third (without a substantial increase of income) would be impossible. However ardently Maud and Lennie might have wished the garden to stay in the family, they must have resigned themselves to the thought that when they died Nymans would be sold to strangers who would sweep away all their work. But in London and elsewhere new ideas were brewing which might offer a solution to the problem.

Several of the historic houses which had come under the protection of the National Trust possessed important gardens, much enjoyed by members of the public, who were visiting the Trust's properties in ever-increasing numbers. It was clear that gardens formed an essential part of Britain's heritage, and that many were at risk. In the years between the wars the biggest social evils had been unemployment and poor working conditions. Outdoor labour was readily available. Wages and other costs remaining remarkably static; agricultural workers were actually paid a little less in 1939 than they had been in 1914. But after the Second World War a new Labour government came into power, bent on improving the lot of the underprivileged masses. Every worker now had to be insured by his employer, other laws were brought in to protect his rights, and wages began to spiral upwards. Inevitably landowners and employers, already hard-pressed by property taxes, were obliged to cut back and 'labour-saving' became the order of the day. Small and medium-sized gardens suffered as much from the stringencies of the times as did the great estates; many of them never recovered from the enforced privations of the war years and were lost for ever. Others desperately needed help if they were to survive at all.

The Royal Horticultural Society, which had so successfully led the way in the 'Dig for Victory' campaign, now turned its attention to helping its members to cope with their post-war problems. Morale was very low, both among the gardening public and within the nursery trade, and here the energetic and forceful ways of the Society's president, Lord Aberconway, were invaluable. He insisted that the Chelsea Show, the great flagship of the Society, should be revived as soon as possible. Although many nurserymen were unenthusiastic at the prospect, saying that they had not had time to build up sufficient stocks of plants to stage worthy exhibits, the first post-war show, in May 1947, was an enormous success. It put heart into everyone who had feared that the old days of high standards and great achievements might never return; in fact against all the odds the art and practice of gardening was about to undergo a great renaissance.

Some horticulturists felt that the National Trust, although doing splendid work on their historic houses, did not possess the necessary resources or expertise to administer gardens in the best way. In November 1947 Lord Aberconway convened a meeting at the Trust's London headquarters to discuss the matter. The RHS membership at that time was more than double that of the National Trust, and Lord Aberconway proposed that the two bodies should form a Joint Committee to administer a selected few important gardens, not necessarily only those which were attached to interesting houses. The fine garden he had particularly in mind was at Hidcote Manor in Gloucestershire; its creator, Lawrence Johnston, was in poor health and since 1943 had intermittently expressed the wish that the National Trust might take over responsibility for his life-work. Although this garden did not exactly fit the Trust's stipulation that their acquisitions should be places of historic interest (it had been formed on an almost featureless piece of land adjoining a small house which Johnston's mother had acquired in 1907), it was a fascinating place, beautifully planted. Hidcote has probably had more influence on the design of modern English gardens than any other, and the thought that it might be altered or go to seed under a new owner was most unwelcome. However, the Trust could not afford to buy Hidcote without help and the problems of upkeep and income (no more than a handful of visitors a week was expected) seemed insurmountable.

It is possible that Lord Aberconway had already discussed the future of Hidcote – and, by inference, Nymans also – with Maud and Lennie. As an old and valued friend he would have been among the first to offer the Messels condolences after the fire, and the welfare of their garden, which he so much admired, would have been much in his mind. He had also consulted Michael, who as a long-time member of both the RHS and the National Trust, and himself the owner of an historic garden, was an ideal person to assist on what was to became known as the Joint Gardens Committee. One of the immediate results of these preliminary discussions was that Lennie wrote a codicil to his will. In this, dated 30 December 1947, he expressed the hope that some member of the family would continue to hold Nymans but, failing that, his trustees were empowered 'to approach some public body or institution to whom the garden would be of interest with a view to acquiring it at a reasonable price or maintaining it at their own expense'. The 'public body' Lennie had in mind could have been none other than the National Trust.

Although Michael must have been delighted that his father-in-law saw the National Trust as a suitable guardian for his last great treasure, he knew that the Trust would have to reject the option of buying Nymans. It was very hard, especially in the early, idealistic days, to refuse interesting properties when it was clear that the alternative to rescue would be annihilation, but over-extension of the Trust's meagre resources was a clear recipe for disaster. Gardens, especially those that were already in decay, were proving just as expensive to maintain as historic houses. Although the tax-saving elements which the government had introduced just before the war were a great help in persuading owners to part with their property, the absolute necessity of providing an endowment of the magnitude that the Trust needed for long-term preservation was still a difficult pill for donors to swallow.

Lord Aberconway clearly understood the doubts and anxieties which beset so many garden owners, but he was determined that his pet project should succeed. He persuaded the RHS to put a substantial sum of money into an Appeal, launched by the Joint Gardens Committee early in 1948, and he campaigned for outside aid at every opportunity.

One idea put forward by a committee member, Vita Sackville-West (whose garden at Sissinghurst Castle, Kent, begun in 1930, was already famous) was that the Queen's Institute for District Nurses – which was just then being incorporated into the new National Health service – might make the National Trust a beneficiary of their very successful Gardens Open Scheme. This came about in 1949 and, although small at first, the Trust's revenue from this source has increased annually. Today, more than 2,500 gardens take part in the National Gardens Scheme and over a million pounds is raised in aid of various charities, approximately a quarter of which is allocated to the National Trust's Garden Fund.

In August 1948, after much havering, Lawrence Johnston finally signed the document giving Hidcote to the National Trust, thus making it the first property to come to them under the Joint Gardens Scheme. Johnston retired to the south of France but he reserved the right to live in the house; he also promised to provide money towards the upkeep of the garden, but this was never adequate. The failure to secure a proper endowment for Hidcote was an error which cost the Trust dear, and it was one they were determined not to repeat.

The future of Nymans remained in doubt for a few more months. Lennie's reluctance to give the property away was perfectly natural: the Messel motto, 'What we have, we hold', was deeply ingrained, and the shock of losing his home and the priceless collections it contained had left a permanent scar. The family fortune, once so large, had dwindled alarmingly since the war, and his first concern was to ensure that Maud and the children were well provided for. Oliver, who had expensive tastes, and Linley, now raising a second family, must have been far from enthusiastic about the dispersal of family assets. Another factor might have made Lennie pause: like many people of his generation, he found the concept of 'tax avoidance' hard to distinguish from 'tax evasion'. He had always been intensely patriotic and the idea of giving something to the National Trust in order to reap tax benefits (thus depriving the government of revenue) would have been unsavoury.

Lennie's nephew, 'young' Eric Parker (another keen gardener, just like his father and grandfather), was consulted on the matter. He had for many years been the family's chief financial adviser and was one of the four executors appointed in Lennie's will. Both he and Michael (also an executor) were anxious to resolve the problem of Nymans in the best possible way. Maud too pressed for a decision: she could see that her husband was making himself ill with worry and needed to know that his garden would fall into good hands. At the end of 1948 arrangements were made for representatives of the RHS and the National Trust to come to Nymans to consider whether it would be possible for the Trust to accept the estate as a gift, should it be offered.

Francis Hanger, formerly Head Gardener at Exbury, but since 1946 Curator of the RHS's garden at Wisley, and Hubert Smith, Chief Agent for the Trust, were the men chosen to make the first report on Nymans. Hanger wrote and lectured on the subject of labour-saving in the garden, but as he walked round Nymans he could see little scope for reducing expenditure. Being largely informal, the garden was not as labour-intensive as some other establishments of comparable size, while new aids which could cut down still further on man-hours, such as weed killers and mechanised garden tools, were still in their infancy and very expensive. Although Hanger suggested that Nymans might acquire a mechanical hedge-clipper he doubted whether even that would be much help. In his report he stated that the garden was certainly 'worthy of preservation', but that money to maintain it would have to depend on the income derived from visitors. As garden-visiting was still a minority occupation, this was hardly a viable option.

Hubert Smith's report reached the same conclusion. Although he wrote, 'The whole estate is well up to National Trust standards', he ended with a strong warning: 'Since no endowment can be provided I fail to see how the Trust could accept this offer without running a very considerable financial risk.'

The Messels were undaunted – perhaps they were not fully informed of the reports' findings – and in February 1949 Lennie finally added the all-important codicil to his will. 'Subject to the National Trust being willing to accept and retain the gift I hereby exclude my said freehold estate hereinafter referred to as Nymans from my residuary estate and bequeath the same to the National Trust to be held by it inalienably for the public benefit in such manner as they may think fit.' He also directed that surplus revenue from the estate was to be used 'to maintain it and particularly the gardens thereof in as perfect a condition as possible', and that Maud (or, failing her, one of the children) should retain the right to occupy the main house. A cottage in the woods was also left for Oliver's use during his lifetime.

Michael, who had been elected to serve on the Council of the National Trust the previous year, reported his father-in-law's decision to it in July. Perhaps to avoid hurting any feelings, the Trust accepted the bequest, but Council was careful to add that it only did so 'subject to the financial arrangements being satisfactory at the time when the gift becomes effective'.

In July 1949 Lord Aberconway asked Michael to lecture to the RHS about the aims of the Joint Committee. Michael told his audience about the work of the National Trust and how it was already responsible for some of the finest gardens in the country, citing Montacute, Packwood, West Wycombe, Blickling, Cliveden, Stourhead, Polesden Lacey, Buscot and Killerton. This was an impressive roll-call but, he stressed, many more gardens were in danger. He described the Trust's first acquisition under the Joint Scheme, Hidcote, in glowing terms, and said that negotiations were even then in progress for the transfer of several other important gardens, although he was not able at that point to disclose their names. Finally, he appealed to all garden lovers to support the new venture.

Later in 1949 Lord Aberconway completed the arrangements for transferring ownership of his own magnificent garden at Bodnant to the National Trust, a noble gesture which did much to raise the horticultural standing of the Trust in the public eye. In this case, although the National Trust became the legal owner, Lord Aberconway and his heirs retained control, both financially and aesthetically, of the way the garden was managed. The Head Gardener, Charles Puddle, who had done so much good work there, stayed on until his retirement and was succeeded in the post by his son, so there was no break in continuity. Nor was it necessary to set up a separate advisory committee, as had been done for Hidcote: this was in trouble from the start, and the many administrative problems there were not solved for years. Bodnant made a wonderful advertisement for the Trust but it was still some time before other garden owners came forward with positive offers or suggestions.

Lennie died at Holmsted Manor on 4 February 1953, a few days before his eighty-first birthday. Although he had been an invalid for a long time, his brother-in-law Eric Parker wrote in *The Times* that the 'bright spirit' of his life-long friend survived unquenched until only an hour or so before the end. The funeral took place at Staplefield and the little church was packed with mourners. Every corner was banked with greenery from the garden that Lennie had loved so much, while the hothouses provided arum lilies and the earliest spring flowers. Maud did not attend owing to illness but the children, grandchildren and an array of cousins came, together with the Messels' many friends from all walks of life. The staff from the house, the garden and the estate were all there – six of the most stalwart carried the coffin – and people from the nearby villages crowded in to pay their respects. The Archdeacon of Lewes preached a sermon of thanksgiving for a long life spent in the service of God and his country, and later a memorial service was held in London. In a letter to *The Times* Lord Aberconway wrote movingly about the great contribution to horticulture made by both Ludwig and Leonard Messel.

James Comber did not long survive his master, dying on 16 May, aged eighty-seven. Once again Staplefield Church was filled with floral tributes, but now it was rhododendron time and flowers of this great gardener's own raising were heaped upon the coffin. Like Lennie, Comber had been a pillar of local society – chairman of Slaugham and Staplefield Horticultural Society, churchwarden at the parish church and Treasurer of the Cricket Club – besides being a generous giver of expert gardening advice to all who asked for it. Although his sphere was narrower than Lennie's, both men were revered throughout the district and their funerals were reported at length in the *Mid-Sussex Times*. Comber was described as 'always upright and distinguished', while Lennie was 'a fine old English gentleman' – an accolade which would have pleased his father. But, as was fitting, Comber the professional gardener received a longer and more fulsome obituary in the *Gardeners' Chronicle* than his employer. Wise and kind, keen and energetic, a valued judge with gardening friends far and wide, were some of the epithets used. All concerned with Nymans had no doubt that his skill and dedication had been major factors in the garden's rise to eminence.

It was indeed the end of an era, as on 23 May 1953 Lord Aberconway died also. But for Nymans there was to be a new beginning. Reluctantly at first, but with slowly gathering commitment, the National Trust took up the challenge of administering this fine garden and its historic collections.

Part III

NYMANS
AND THE
NATIONAL TRUST

Chapter Ten

The National Trust

Within a fortnight of Lennie's death the National Trust's Chief Agent had visited Nymans and compiled another report for Head Office. A cold and dismal February day is not the most heartening time to view a garden and Hubert Smith felt that nothing had improved since his previous visit, also in midwinter, four years earlier. Lack of a strong guiding hand since then showed up the shortcomings of the garden; the various farms and cottages on the estate were in poor shape and rents were absurdly low. The ruins of the big house – which dominated the southern half of the pleasure grounds – presented, to his eyes, 'a most depressing picture'. It was possible that members of the family might want to live in the reconstructed wing (work here was still in progress), but the rest would certainly have to be demolished. In short, Smith was not in favour of Nymans coming to the Trust.

Clearly something had to be done if the garden was to be preserved in the way that Lord Aberconway and the Messel family had hoped. Complicated negotiations ensued between the National Trust and Lennie's executors. The latter would have been hard pressed to find sufficient funds to pay the death duties on the estate should the Trust refuse the bequest, so that the additional gift of an endowment might go some way towards solving everyone's problems. In May it was settled that £20,000, invested at $4\frac{1}{2}$ per cent, would be donated. At that time the rate of inflation, although creeping upwards, had not become rampant and £20,000 was a considerable sum of money; even so, many at the Trust were uncertain whether it would be sufficient for the property to be well run. However, the doubters on the committee were over-ruled and the Secretary wrote to Eric Parker, 'We all realize that without the great generosity of the family in offering £20,000 endowment it would have been impossible for the Trust to accept Colonel Messel's devise . . . would you please convey to the family the Trust's great gratitude for their generosity and support in making possible the preservation of these gardens.'

The acquisition of Nymans by the National Trust was announced at a press conference in September 1953. The following year its name was added to the list of twenty-one gardens which were run by the Trust, and open to the public at a cost of 1s. or 2s. per head. (The annual membership subscription at the time was 10s.) The desirability of private houses and gardens coming into the public domain was as much under discussion at that time as it is today. The policies of the Trust were often criticised, especially the general 'cleaning up' and sanitising operations which were often no more than desperate necessity. One newspaper article referred to 'the dead hand of the National Trust', and this became a catch-phrase among those who opposed its work. In response the Trust went to great lengths to try to avoid a blanket uniformity overtaking its properties. They found it less easy to preserve individuality in the houses than in the gardens; the type of restoration favoured at this time, the colours and styles of decoration, were dominated by a small coterie of interior designers with a predilection for the newly fashionable eighteenth century. Gardens escaped their influence, and head gardeners were usually acknowledged as experts on their own patch. Although the Trust held the purse-strings the head gardener could say how many men he thought were needed to work the place, what materials should to be bought in, and what would be the major planting plans each year. This state of affairs was usually quite satisfactory, and the Trust has been remarkably well served by its gardeners. Even so, as an article in the RHS *Journal* at this time pointed out, 'when the guidance and pressure of the instigator's thumb are removed, though the garden may still have well trimmed hedges and well groomed lawns, the best of the plant material suffers.' For this reason the National Trust has always welcomed any personal interest and concern shown by former owners and their relatives. In Nymans' case, Michael's close involvement with both the Trust's general garden policy and the Messel family was regarded as a welcome bonus.

The Trust's land agent for the south-east region was Ivan Hills, who worked from an office in another historic house, Polesden Lacey in Surrey. Everyone knew from the start that money would be tight at Nymans, and Hills' instructions were to save every penny. This was not an easy task as wherever he looked he could see evidence of gross neglect. The first difficulty was with the old-age pensioners: Maud upheld their right to continue paying tiny rents, even though these went no way towards meeting the alterations necessary to make their tumbledown cottages comply with the post-war standards demanded by the local council. Hills was obliged to insist that the tenants be moved into alternative accommodation; the Trust then repaired the properties and re-let at higher rents, actions which did not endear them to the local population. It soon became clear that the limits of National Trust authority were insufficiently defined: responsibility for the upkeep of the main house, as well as of Oliver's cottage, became a bone of contention. It has always been a point of honour with the Trust that any remaining family should not feel cast out from their old home, but when personal feelings are strong it is inevitable that disagreements of this kind will arise.

Maud's Edwardian attitudes, her dreamy voice and unfinished sentences, quite nonplussed outsiders who tried to apply modern ideas to the administration of a run-down estate. It was therefore decided that family interests would be best served if Anne and Michael, rather than Maud, dealt with the garden. The National Trust's Secretary, Jack Rathbone, wrote to Hills, 'As with Lord Aberconway at Bodnant, Lord Rosse is responsible to the Gardens Committee for the management of Nymans, although of course there will be a greater degree of delegation to us than at Bodnant.' However, things were to turn out a little differently: Anne and Michael proceeded to treat the place as if it were their own, issuing directions and ignoring proffered advice. To Ivan Hills their intervention was not entirely welcome, and he reported to the Chief Agent that it seemed impossible to get the simplest thing done at Nymans, so many different people had to be consulted. Those at Head Office were more grateful: as the success of the whole venture was clearly close to the Rosses' hearts, the Trust felt absolved from worry or the need to plan ahead. With good luck and good management all the present difficulties would soon be overcome.

At Nymans Anne and Michael established a base in the restored section of the old house, which they used between visits to their other homes, and Anne pleased her mother by fostering the paternalism which had been so much a part of the old way of life. Her assumption that the garden staff were all still loyal Messel retainers sometimes caused trouble (the Trust was not always pleased to find that their employees served two masters), but it was mainly through her influence that Nymans retained for so long the atmosphere of a private garden and much-loved family home.

A formal opening ceremony for the garden was held on Friday, 6 March 1954. It was a beautiful afternoon; Colonel Ralph Stephenson Clarke from Borde Hill (son of Ludwig's old friend, Stephenson R. Clarke) presided, and Vita Sackville-West – representing the Joint

Lady Rosse in the saloon, Birr Castle, by her son, Tony Armstrong-Jones

Gardens Committee – declared the gardens open. Maud, Linley, Anne and Oliver were all there, and Anne made a speech. It was, she said, not a sad occasion for the family. It had been her father's dearest wish that the future of Nymans should be assured: a garden need lose none of its intimate, romantic or even sentimental values by being shared with others, rather the reverse. Some of her father's happiest hours had been spent escorting parties round the garden on summer afternoons. If, in days to come, those who visited Nymans derived from what they saw not only pleasure but inspiration, and if that inspiration developed to benefit the world of horticulture as a whole, then her father's and grandfather's greatest desires would be accomplished and their work would not have been in vain.

The National Trust proposed more generous opening hours than when Nymans had been a private estate: Tuesdays, Wednesdays, Thursdays and Sundays, 2 p.m. to 7 p.m., from the beginning of April to the end of October. Admission was 2s. However, no extra facilities were provided to tempt more visitors to come to the garden; cars could park in the drive but there was no entrance kiosk (not even a shelter for the ticket collector if it rained), no guide book, and no place for refreshments. All these were very slow in coming and though the family was pleased by the first influx of visitors, numbers soon fell away and the Trust was grievously disappointed. It had been hoped that sales of produce from the kitchen garden would show enough profit to support the pleasure grounds, but only £560 was raised this way, just over half the estimate. The bad weather that summer was blamed for the poor start and hopes were pinned on the next season, with the kitchen garden being able to increase sales and make up any deficit.

Since James Comber's death Cecil Nice had become Head Gardener in fact, not name only, and his transference to Comber's cottage, one of the best on the estate, set the seal on his authority. Aged forty-eight when the National Trust took over, he worked well and tirelessly for his new masters for the rest of his life, but he never had the drive and vision of his predecessor, nor was he ever encouraged, either by them or by the Rosses, to develop initiatives. The kitchen garden was his special pride and he assured the Trust that it could be made profitable; certainly over the next few years the output increased and quite a good income was generated. But it was not enough: all over the country old-fashioned walled gardens, which had been so successful in a previous era, when not just labour but boiler fuel and horse manure were cheap and plentiful, were in trouble. In spite of all Nice's efforts the sale of produce from the kitchen garden did not cover the shortfall in the pleasure grounds.

The first guide book for Nymans was ready by the beginning of the 1955 season. Anne made a drawing for the cover and also wrote the text: this was a slightly modified version of an article entitled 'Nymans Gardens', illustrated with black-and-white photographs by her son Tony, which she had written for the April 1953 issue of the RHS *Journal*. With only minor alterations, this guide book was to serve the visitors for over thirty years. Opening times for the garden were advertised in the local paper and a new directional sign was erected in Handcross, but visitor numbers continued to be very disappointing, actually falling from the previous year's figure of 3,373 to 2,804.

The National Trust had acquired another fine Sussex garden in 1954: Arthur Soames's Sheffield Park. On Soames's death in 1934 the estate had passed to his nephew, who lived there for twenty years before making a sudden decision to sell up. On hearing this news, the Trust launched an appeal and, although insufficient money was raised to secure the magnificent house, the landscaped park, with its pedigree stretching back to Capability Brown, was saved from the housing development that had been threatened. After the familiar initial struggles to counter wartime neglect, Sheffield Park became one of the National Trust's most successful properties, the only garden to contribute a healthy surplus to the Gardens Fund. Its rapidly mounting visitor figures proved what many at Head Office already knew: members of the public would come for miles, not just once but regularly and often, for a chance to enjoy a fine landscape set-piece. The lakes, the carefully composed views, the bold sheets of colour – from daffodils or rhododendrons in their season – and the splendid trees, all appealed to a wide spectrum of garden lovers. Sheffield Park had been specially planted for autumn effects: in October and November, when other gardens had little to show, it was a blaze of glory.

By contrast the smaller, more specialist gardens, such as Nymans and Tintinhull in Somerset (which also came to the Trust in 1954), consistently failed to draw big crowds; even Hidcote was not much visited in the early days. Vita Sackville-West's articles in the *Observer* about her garden at Sissinghurst, published between 1946 and 1960, did much to open people's eyes to the beauty of individual flowers, but the public's greatest admiration was usually reserved for the eighteenth-century type of landscape garden as perfected by Brown and Repton; if this had later been embellished with large slabs of colour, so much the better. 'Garden history' as a serious academic study was still in the future – nobody complained in the 1950s, as they did thirty years later, about the inappropriateness of the rhododendrons at Stourhead. Not surprisingly, the National Trust was tempted to spend only a small proportion of its limited funds on its less popular places, and more on garden staff and visitor facilities for the larger properties. At these, car parks, lavatories and tea-rooms were followed, as demand grew, by shops, plant centres and exhibition spaces.

Nymans, only a few miles away from Sheffield Park, was not considered a good candidate for such expenditure. As had happened at Hidcote, the Trust's original estimates for running the garden turned out to be wildly optimistic. Inflation, especially the steep rise in gardeners' wages, took everyone by surprise. With each year that passed the accounts at Nymans went further into the red: labour costs and essential repairs far outweighed the income accrued from visitors, rents and invested capital. Thus Ivan Hills was under constant pressure to make economies and to cut back wherever possible: repairs were kept to an absolute minimum, as was the garden staff, and even requests for small necessities – a new wheelbarrow or a ladder – were turned down. This naturally had an adverse effect on morale: con-

The Italian fountain surrounded by luxuriant growth, making the 'secret garden' effect so much loved by Anne

vinced of the beauty and importance of their garden, all those concerned with its welfare found the Trust's penny-pinching attitude most
distressing.

The small number of visitors could be ascribed to many reasons. As
even basic amenities were lacking the hoped-for coachloads of tourists
from the coastal resorts (already such a feature at Bodnant that a large
car park had to be built to accommodate them) naturally failed to
materialise. Added to this was the incontrovertible fact that Nymans
was a true garden-lover's garden. Its subtleties and complexities, the
major contributions made by the Messels to the history of gardening,
were concepts not easily grasped by ordinary families who came for a
pleasant afternoon out. Rare plants do not always have exciting flowers
– their appeal is mainly to botanists and hybridists – and Anne's guide
book, although a pleasurable read for the connoisseur and full of Latin
names, was too difficult for most people to understand. Nymans is, in
the main, a wild garden; Robinsonian principles allow for a certain
number of weeds and those who expected to find a formal layout,
manicured to perfection, were sometimes critical of the more casual
approach.

Of course, from the first Nymans had its own band of devotees.
There were those who came especially to see the rhododendrons,
others for whom the spring-flowering trees were the great draw. In
July and August there was the colourful border in the Wall Garden to
admire, as well as fine displays of hydrangeas and eucryphias. But it
seems that those who loved Nymans best and visited it most often were
not primarily concerned with any of these things. For them it was the
special atmosphere of peace and seclusion, the secret places and
half-hidden delights, the unexpected glories, that meant so much. The
shaded walks between banks of evergreens, the sudden shafts of
sunlight and tantalising glimpses of a distant view, the grim ruin
garlanded with flowers, all contributed to a romantic vision very
different from the wide vistas of Sheffield Park.

Graham Stuart Thomas was appointed Horticultural Advisor to the
National Trust in 1955. This was at first a low-paid job which Thomas
expected to be able to do in his spare time, his main employment being
with a firm of Surrey nurserymen. Although his original brief was to
advise on four gardens only (soon extended to cover twelve more) he
never became a full-time employee of the Trust, and did all his work
from home. He had known Nymans since the 1930s and was an
admirer, not only of Maud's roses, but of the multitude of other
interesting plants in the garden. He was not, however, so enthusiastic

about the form and layout of the place; like many others at that time he longed to cut and prune, feeling that sunlight and views should take precedence over the Messels' preference for shady seclusion. Thus his first advisory visit to Nymans in July 1955 was not an unqualified success; he found the Rosses unwilling to fall in with any of his suggestions and adamant that no trees – not even the most ragged and ailing conifer – should be taken down. His report to Head Office was critical of many things, not least the hazards he foresaw of divided rule in the garden.

Both the Messel family and the National Trust (proud of its reputation as the guardian of excellence) thought it essential that Nymans should retain its position as a place of pilgrimage for connoisseurs and a source of interesting new plants. The RHS fortnightly shows in Vincent Square had quickly got back into their stride after the war, with Nymans' old friends and rivals – Bodnant, Caerhays, Leonardslee, Borde Hill, South Lodge, Exbury – still leaders of the pack when it came to awards. These gardens continued to be run as family concerns, some of them entering into their third generation of dedicated plantsmen-owners. Wakehurst Place had passed out of the Loder family but its new owner, Sir Henry Price, was another great gardener who enjoyed showing off his treasures. It was time for Nymans to re-enter the race, especially as everyone there was convinced they had some likely prize-winners among the many young trees and shrubs which Lennie and Comber had bred and nurtured during their last years.

The most promising of these was a magnolia. *Magnolia × loebneri* was the name given to a cross first made in Germany in 1910 between the bushy, dwarf *M. stellata* and the tall *M. kobus*. Loebner's work was repeated by several breeders and the resultant hybrids grew into slender trees, tolerant of alkaline soil (unlike many magnolias) and well set with blossom. At Nymans the reverse cross had taken place by chance: an unusual variety of *M. kobus* with a pale purple line on each tepal was pollinated with *M. stellata* 'Rosea'. In the new hybrid, quantities of deep reddish-pink buds expanded to 5 inch flowers, creamy-white inside, giving from a distance an overall colouring of pale pink. Confident that here was a plant of exceptional merit, the family named it 'Leonard Messel'. In May 1955, described as coming from 'Mrs L.C.R. Messel and the National Trust', it received an Award of Merit (upgraded in 1969 to a First Class Certificate) at Vincent Square. Never growing very large and more resistant to frost damage than the white-flowered forms, *Magnolia* 'Leonard Messel' has proved to be one of the most successful ornamental trees introduced since the war. The fact that it flowers generously even when pot-sized has made it a best seller, especially in the garden centres which have largely replaced mail order during the last twenty years. It has easily outpaced Nymans' earlier claim to fame, *Eucryphia* 'Nymansay', which, in spite of its virtues, is not suited to the modern garden where space is at a premium.

Two other Awards of Merit went to Nymans in 1955: one for *Rhododendron anthopogon* and another for *Desfontainia spinosa* 'Harold Comber'. Encouraged by these successes, Nymans' attendance at Vincent Square once again became a regular event. Numerous medals and awards were won each year, for groups of flowering plants as well as for individual specimens.

In 1958 the garden had another splendid hybrid of its own raising ready to show. Several of the new race of *Camellia × williamsii*, bred by J. C. Williams at Caerhays, had found their way to Nymans. Lennie had been particularly interested in these and, during the war – when there were no gardeners available to do anything but the most pressing tasks – had himself experimented with hybridisation. He crossed 'Mary Christian' (named for Mrs Williams) with *Camellia reticulata*, a slightly tender species with particularly large and luscious blooms. The result-ant seedlings looked very promising, although sadly Lennie did not live to see them at their best. One was selected and, like the magnolia, named after him by his devoted family. Shown at Vincent Square, *Camellia* 'Leonard Messel' was awarded an Award of Merit in 1958, a First Class Certificate in 1970 and the Cory Cup in 1971. It inherits the tough constitution of 'Mary Christian', growing about 10 feet tall and opening early in the season; its beautiful semi-double flowers, rich pink with prominent stamens, are borne with the greatest profusion. Grafted and distributed by Waterers, it proved very successful, particu-larly in America, where it won many first prizes at camellia shows. Although there has been a spate of camellia introductions in recent years, 'Leonard Messel' is still considered one of the best of the post-war hybrids.

The annual deficit at Nymans continued to rise and the Trust's Chief Agent was firmly of the opinion that only an increased endowment could solve the problem. Unfortunately, nobody felt able to say outright to any member of the family that the current financial arrangements were insufficient. Michael was usually optimistic and briskly dismissive of difficulties, while there was a tacit agreement that Maud, whose health was increasingly precarious, should not be

Maud Messel in old age, taken by her grandson, Tony Armstrong-Jones

worried. Hubert Smith called on her in January 1960: this seems to have been the first time that he felt able to speak perfectly frankly to her about the situation at Nymans and, contrary to his expectations, she grasped the problem at once. Distressed to hear what a drain the property was to the Trust, Maud suggested closing down the vegetable garden and leaving the wild part of the pleasure grounds to its own devices. This would cut the staff from ten gardeners to five, a major saving at a time when agricultural wages were increasing annually. Such a plan would have directly countered Michael's wishes which were to extend the garden, take on more staff and increase the sale of produce from the kitchen garden.

Sadly, Maud became seriously ill before her proposal could be discussed but it seems clear that had she been more closely involved in the early stages some far-reaching economies might have been arranged and a proper investment plan for the future drawn up. Instead Michael's counsel prevailed and Nymans was allowed to stuggle on, the staff urged to raise standards of upkeep while 'making do' with poor equipment. Ivan Hills' file is full of the usual land agent's problems – fallen trees, leaking roofs, rents not paid and so on – but one senses an increasing feeling of desperation about his, and the National Trust's, failure to make Nymans financially viable.

Maud died, aged eighty-four, on 8 March 1960. The family felt her loss acutely: Anne and Oliver especially had idolised their mother all their lives, and the grandchildren adored her. The obituary which appeared in *The Times* the following day must have been written by someone who knew her well. It spoke with respect of her girlhood spent among well-known artists and intellectuals, of her own talents and especially of her beauty. 'In her later years Mrs Messel was more than the legendary great lady of an archaic past. Certainly her exquisite manner and presence belonged to a different age from ours. Her iridiscent, almost gossamer-like beauty was that of the tenderly nurtured exotic rather than of the wild hedgerow flower. Her sad and gentle voice, however, spoke from the depths of unfeigned compassion and understanding. And beneath her apparent fragility lay a strength of character, an invincibility of courage, and an insatiable fund of interest in all around her. Her contemporaries and younger friends did not find these qualities surprising in one whose whole life was dedicated to a love of human beings, as well as of nature and art.'

The funeral service was held at Staplefield Church. Once again this was filled with family and friends, as well as representatives of all the local charities which Maud had supported during her long life. The

Mid-Sussex Times devoted almost as much space to her passing as it had to Lennie's, but there was an additional reason for newspaper interest: Maud's grandson, Tony Armstrong-Jones, was among the mourners and his engagement to Princess Margaret had just been announced. All the world wanted to know about this young man's antecedents, so the Messels, and Nymans too, were more in the public eye than they had ever been before.

Tony was married in Westminster Abbey on 6 May 1960. His extended family (Ronald had recently married for the third time) were all invited and the order of seating for his closest relations posed some knotty problems for the organisers. At Nymans the garden staff were given the day off, and beer, so that they could drink the happy couple's health while watching the great event on television. For everyone in sleepy Handcross the excitement must have been intense as the cameras lingered on the familiar figures occupying the front pews of the Abbey, then roamed across a sea of faces – Michael, Oliver, Tony's sister Susan, his half-brothers and his cousins who had played at Nymans in their childhood – all mingling with the highest in the land. Anne and Ronald sat together for the service, then walked down the aisle behind the Royal party to drive in procession through cheering crowds to Buckingham Palace. Neither Tony nor Princess Margaret had grand-

Lord Rosse in the drawing room at
18 Stafford Terrace, London

parents to wish them joy, and all at Nymans must have felt regret that
Maud had missed the great occasion by so narrow a margin. Eighteen
months later Tony was created Earl of Snowdon, with the subsidiary
title of Viscount Linley of Nymans.

On Maud's death Anne inherited the London house at 18 Stafford
Terrace which had belonged to her grandparents, Linley and Marion
Sambourne. Sentimentally devoted to the memory of her happy
childhood, Maud had helped her bachelor brother Roy (who lived there
all his life) to keep the house in good order. He had died in 1946,
leaving everything to her, but as she could not bear to part with the
house she had encouraged Anne and Michael to make use of it. The
interior, furnished in the 'aesthetic' mode of the 1870s, had by now
almost the appearance of a stage set. The Rosses found it a wonderful
place for entertaining and greatly enjoyed seeing the reactions of their
friends – some horrified, others enchanted – when they crossed the
threshold. In the post-war rush to modernise Britain, Victorian
buildings and their contents were being ruthlessly swept away: most
people were convinced that everything Victorian was hopelessly outmoded, its art and architecture of little interest to serious connoisseurs.
The Rosses believed otherwise and in 1957 Anne suggested that a
society, like the Georgian Group, should be formed to campaign for
the preservation and appreciation of another great period in British
history. The idea took root and several friends who shared her enthusiasm –
John Betjeman, Nikolaus Pevsner, Hugh Casson, Viscount Esher, Mark
Girouard and Ian Grant among them – were invited to a party at 18 Stafford
Terrace in February 1958. Here, surrounded by her grandfather's pictures
and *objets d'art*, Anne founded the Victorian Society.

Chapter Eleven

Historic Gardens and their Care

A t Nymans Anne formally adopted the position of 'Director' of the garden in 1960. She assumed Maud's mantle in other ways, too, chiefly by bringing Messel relatives together and insisting that Nymans remained an important focus of family pride. But the Rosses now had little reason to spend much time in Sussex and some friction between them and the National Trust officials inevitably developed. Both Anne and Michael were blithe spenders, accustomed all their lives to having the best of everything. Their wedding presents to one another typify their attitudes: he had given her a magnificent set of emeralds and she had presented Birr Castle with a suite of Chippendale furniture. They entertained lavishly, drawing their friends from the worlds of art, architecture and the theatre; Michael sat on numerous committees and was much admired for his erudition and tact. At Nymans it was the vision of the founder and the plethora of rare plants which were vitally important, not the gate-money. The Rosses would descend on the garden for a brief visit, go into raptures over its beauty, issue a few directives, then depart in a whirl for their next destination. For those who had to deal with day-to-day problems, and balance the books, such a regime was not easy. Anne in particular was opposed to any change in the way the garden was run and she determined to stand firm against what she saw as the creeping materialism of the Trust.

Anne was all her life a passionate devotee of the past: nothing in the garden must be altered, not a tree felled, not a bend in the path straightened. Sentiment, romance, atmosphere – these were key words in her vocabulary. It is right that people should take such feelings into acount: Anne preached her doctrine tirelessly to all who came within her orbit and thereby made a valuable contribution, not only to Nymans but to the whole conservation debate. Michael had more of an eye for practicalities and his counsel often prevailed when others found Anne too intransigent. However, neither of them seemed to be able to look really far ahead and decide what shape the garden should have in fifty years' time, when all Ludwig's plantings would have reached the end of their natural span.

Although major change might be resisted, a continual progression of minor improvements and necessary renewal is essential for the proper maintenance of any garden. This the Rosses encouraged, and they were especially keen that both Birr and Nymans should continue to be in the forefront of gardens associated with new plant discoveries. To this end they kept up the pre-war tradition of subscribing to various expeditions. In China, Dr Hu's collecting from 1937–40 resulted in several interesting plants coming to Birr, and the Cox–Hutchinson expedition to Assam in 1965 brought new rhododendrons and primulas. Exchanges between the two gardens were encouraged: young plants of *Sophora microphylla*, *Meliosma cuneifolia*, *Itea ilicifolia* and several varieties of ceanothus – all successful in Ireland – were taken to Sussex where they found the different climate and soil conditions much to their liking. Some unusual conifers were propagated and donated to Nymans also. Among several hybrids raised at Birr was a paeony, a cross between *P. lutea ludlowii* and *P. delavayi*. This had 4 inch lemon yellow flowers streaked with red and was named 'Anne Rosse'. In July 1961 it won an Award of Merit from the RHS; at the Society's AGM the following February Michael was presented with the Cory Cup. As this was the first time that the cup had ever gone to Ireland, the Rosses were especially pleased.

Anne was particularly keen on camellias. She and Michael brought back cuttings from holidays spent in Portugal, with Muriel Tait, who had a fine garden at Quinta do Meio, and the United States, where many exciting new varieties were coming on the market. Two large wooden crates of cuttings arrived at Nymans one weekend and instructions were issued, somewhat to the gardeners' displeasure, to pot them up at once. The old laurels round the Sunk Garden were replaced with a mixture of these camellias which soon made a splendid feature at the southern end of the garden in spring. However, the early part of the year had always been the best time for a visit to Nymans and although some thought had been devoted to the problem of providing more colour during the summer months, there were still blank periods when the public might justifiably feel some disappointment.

Graham Stuart Thomas was certainly disappointed. He paid Nymans a visit at the end of June 1963 and at once sent off a strongly worded criticism to Ivan Hills. 'For one of our principal gardens to be so dull at the crown of the year is a disgrace and an admission of failure . . . I do not feel that we should tolerate such neglect,' he wrote. His opinion was conveyed, less bluntly, to the Rosses and as a result a 'June Border' containing lilies, meconopsis and primulas, paeonies, irises, lupins and delphiniums was created in the Top Garden. Some of these plants were also added to the borders on the south side of the house. The Rose Garden was overhauled too: here much of Maud's original conception was now untidy and overgrown – besides, her planting had been more for sentiment than for colourful display. Graham Thomas's advice was taken over selecting the best old-fashioned roses and some iron arches and pillars were introduced to give height and variety. Great improvements also took place in the Pinetum which instead of being fenced off, as before, was made accessible to visitors. Cut glades and mown paths intersected it, plantings of rhododendrons and azaleas nearby were extended, and more eucryphias were added in the gaps. Lennie had already planted hydrangeas to add autumn interest to the garden: 'Blue Wave', 'Veitchii', 'Europa' and others had done very well, so it was decided to enlarge the clumps and make them a real feature.

All these alterations took place after a major upheaval in the way the garden was run. Every year the National Trust's Gardens Committee expressed grave concern about the increasing deficit at Nymans. This had risen to over £2,000 in 1961; at the same time Hidcote's deficit had been reduced to £219 and Sheffield Park was showing a small profit. Early in 1962 the energetic new chairman of the committee, Dr (later Sir) George Taylor, the Director of Kew Gardens, had called for all interested parties to attend a meeting at Nymans to discuss what might be done to improve the situation. The axing of the kitchen garden was one possibility which took high priority. Although Anne, Michael and Cecil Nice fought hard for its retention they were forced to bow to the combined weight of Trust opinion. Economic pressures were such that the revenue it brought in did not justify the number of staff employed to keep it going, and the time spent by the head gardener on organising the sale of produce could be used to better effect in that part of the garden which was open to the public.

It was a great wrench for those who had known Nymans for so long to part with the kitchen garden, in the past always considered the mainspring of a country estate. Within its perimeter lay the tool store and potting shed, the propagating house, the cold frames and all the paraphernalia essential for raising not only fruit and vegetables but also the young stock for the pleasure grounds. Some of this equipment

Lord and Lady Rosse with Cecil Nice in the Wall Garden, 1975

would still be needed and two old greenhouses in the Top Garden (one of which had been given over to Lennie's collection of terrestrial orchids in the 1930s) could be adapted to form an administration centre, with a new propagating shed and boiler house, and a small office. This would leave the gardener's cottage somewhat isolated, so it was decided that a new house for Cecil Nice should be built on the west side of the main garden, close to the gates and the existing lodge, thus enabling the whole of the old kitchen garden complex to be let on lease. (Nymans was an inalienable estate, so no part of it could be sold.) The Trust's Finance Committee agreed that a sum of £4,000 could be spent the following year on building work.

Once the changes had been made and assimilated, everyone expressed themselves very pleased with the arrangements. Cecil Nice was able to move into his new house in January 1964 and the administrative centre was in full working order by the spring. Although the adaptation of the old glasshouses was rather makeshift there were clear advantages in having everything close together near the centre of the garden, one being that the staff, reduced to six men, wasted less time walking to and from their various tasks. The kitchen garden had been some distance from the main house, and visitors today are not aware that it was ever part of the estate. (The cottage was renamed 'Combers', but the luxuriant growth around it, so lovingly cultivated by generations of professional gardeners, has now been shorn away.) Most importantly, the interest shown in Nymans' affairs by Head Office – and the injection of cash – was a great boost to staff morale. In the next few years many people, both members of the public and visiting Trust officials, commented very favourably on the improved state of the gardens.

Plants from Nymans, since 1960 exhibited under the banner of 'The National Trust and the Countess of Rosse', continued to win prizes, both at the RHS and elsewhere. A fine display of hydrangeas was given a Gold Medal at the Brighton Flower Show in 1963 and a Silver Banksian Medal (also for hydrangeas) was won at Chelsea in 1964. The most successful year of this decade was 1966, when thirty-three prizes were won in the various Shrub and Rhododendron classes at Vincent Square, eleven of them being firsts. A *Rhododendron brachyanthum* hybrid was given an AM and Anne named this, too, after her father, achieving a long-held ambition to have him remembered in the three great plant families – magnolia, camellia and rhododendron – which he had loved best.

National Trust membership continued to rise. By the end of 1965, the year that Enterprise Neptune – the great appeal for the preservation of the coastline – was launched, it stood at 157,581 (twenty times greater than in 1945). Since the war leisure time had increased enormously and car ownership was no longer exclusive to the rich. Driving around to look at the countryside, going for walks, or visiting other people's houses and gardens, were popular pastimes. By the mid-1960s the Trust's Country Houses Scheme was not only well established but extending its scope, while the preservation of gardens was acknowledged as an important issue. Two significant gardens were acquired in south-east England in the 1960s: Wakehurst Place and Sissinghurst Castle. They were in good order when taken over and posed few management problems. Wakehurst was leased to the Royal Botanic Gardens, Kew, who became responsible for its administration, and Sissinghurst was cared for by two expert gardeners who had worked under its creator, Vita Sackville-West. Both gardens quickly went close to the top of the Trust's list of most-visited properties.

The rapid growth of garden visiting naturally led to the development of a more critical approach to the making and maintaining of all gardens, whether private or public. After the war the planting of large ornamental trees and shrubs was deemed impractical; besides, the great age of exploration and plant-hunting was over and no dramatic new finds became available. The dedicated plantsman and enthusiastic searcher after rarities was not, as in the past, a rich man with broad acres and numerous staff, but was now more likely to be the owner of a small patch of ground worked entirely by himself. Labour saving was thus more important than ever: 'ground cover' was recommended for the modern garden and Graham Stuart Thomas's development of this idea at several National Trust properties was largely responsible for the concept being widely taken up.

The horticultural world has always had its specialist societies, formed in response to prevailing fashions. The Hardy Plant Society (founded in 1957) was devoted to the rediscovery of those herbaceous plants which had been rather neglected during the years between the wars when shrub gardening had been in the ascendant. The Garden History Society (founded in 1966) marked a resurgence of interest in the layout and planting of old gardens. Detailed and painstaking research into garden archaeology, going as far back as Roman times, opened people's eyes to a whole new discipline. Books on gardening began to proliferate; purely instructive 'how to dig' manuals were the bestsellers, but these were gradually augmented by books on garden design (both old and new) and the history of plant collections.

Visitor numbers at Nymans continued to increase every year but they still lagged behind those at other Trust gardens of comparable size. The continuing lack of even basic amenities was a great handicap. Cars, tightly packed along both drives on busy Sundays, damaged the grass verges and spoilt the peaceful character of the garden. Although ice-cream and cups of tea were obtainable from a small hut in the grounds the service was erratic and unsatisfactory. Plans for a proper tea-room and car park had been on and off the agenda for years but no ideal site for either existed. One suggestion was that land on the opposite side of the road could be levelled to make space for cars, but this was vetoed by the County Council as being too dangerous for pedestrians. The alternative was a large empty paddock, formerly used as a cricket field, which lay at the northern end of the estate. It was considered rather too far from the heart of the garden to be ideal but it was well screened by trees and allowed plenty of room for expansion if necessary. In January 1966 the Trust's General Purposes Committee agreed to grant money for some much-needed improvements. Half the cricket field was to be used for parking (with a lavatory block at one side), the other half made into a new entrance garden, with a path leading from it into the Top Garden. A new tea-room was still deemed too much of an extravagance, so the refreshment hut carried on as before.

The car park, ready for use in 1967, was most welcome as far as convenience was concerned but there was one major snag: by entering from the north the whole sequence of viewing the garden was in the reverse order from that intended by its creator. This is a problem encountered at some properties open to visitors – the public is obliged to creep into the great house by way of a side door, the finest rooms left until the end. Gardens suffer in the same way: at Nymans the Top Garden had always been a place for plants which could not be fitted in elsewhere, while the greenhouses and tool sheds of the administrative centre, formerly tucked out of sight, made an obtrusive group beside what was now one of the main ways through the garden. Anne, as usual, would not tolerate more change than was absolutely essential and no outside design expert was consulted. Lanning Roper (who did excellent work at Chartwell, altering the paths to make the garden accessible and attractive to a large number of visitors) might have done much for Nymans: as it was, a few shrubs round the new entrance was all that could be managed.

A revised edition of the guide book, with colour photographs, set out the new route for visitors. On entering the Top Garden they were encouraged to turn left into the Pinetum, walk down the slope and approach the house by the lime avenue on the western boundary. They were then to work round the southern parts of the estate – the Sunk Garden, the Heath Garden, the lawns and pergola – and return to the car park through the Wall Garden. This makes an attractive tour but rather a long one, the steep slope at the beginning being a disincentive to the elderly. Many visitors preferred to stroll along the level north-south axis path through the Wall Garden, make a short circuit of the lawns, and then go back the same way. The predictable result was that large tracts of the pleasure grounds went relatively unexplored, while the Wall Garden with its colourful summer borders – much photographed and admired – was sometimes badly overcrowded.

As expected, the improved parking facilities attracted more visitors, over 17,000 by the end of 1969. This was a matter for some congratulation, but two programmes on *Gardener's World*, presented by Percy Thrower in May and August 1971, caused numbers to leap to 41,000. Even though this figure fell back to 28,000 in 1972 it showed what a little publicity in the right place could do. A large number of the visitors, when questioned, said that they had known about Nymans for a long time but had not thought it worth while making a visit until told to do so on television.

Daffodils in the park at Nymans

Behind the scenes other important work was carried on. In 1970 a three-year task of identifying and recording all the species rhododendrons, in both the garden and the old nursery ground (now called 'The Rough') was concluded. Rhododendron seed is known to be very variable: one of Kingdon-Ward's best introductions was *R. macabeanum*, found in 1927. Dozens of this plant grew at Nymans, and they varied considerably in form and colour, some being of a much better habit or a purer yellow than others. Although many of the nursery plants had been swamped by undergrowth, others had matured into fine specimens, quite distinct from anything known to exist elsewhere. Dr Harold Fletcher, secretary of the International Commission for the Nomenclature of Cultivated Plants, suggested that all these rhododendrons should be properly identified. John Clarke and Alan Hardy, both keen amateur enthusiasts, volunteered to help Cecil Nice with this monumental task on one afternoon a week. Many of the original labels had been lost and much careful detective work was needed: details of the labour involved were published in the *Rhododendron and Camellia Year Book* of 1970 and 1971. Thus Nymans became the first garden to possess a complete catalogue of natural-source rhododendron species, an achievement of real scientific importance. As a result, several learned foundations asked to be supplied with material to augment their collections.

In February 1970 Cecil Nice was presented with the Waley Medal by the RHS. This, awarded to a working gardener who has helped in the cultivation of rhododendrons, was well deserved: Nymans' regular successes at the shows since the war owed much to its head gardener's skills in both raising and showing these plants. Everyone was delighted also when *Rhododendron pocophorum* 'Cecil Nice' was given an Award of Merit in March 1971. Other good plants continued to come out of Nymans. In 1968 *Magnolia* 'Michael Rosse', a cross between *M. campbellii* and *M. sargentiana*, with large flowers of soft purple-pink, received an Award of Merit. This is very lovely but has not found its way into many gardens: it certainly deserves to be better known. In 1970 *Camellia* 'Maud Messel' (from the same parentage as *C.* 'Leonard Messel' but earlier-flowering with small shapely pink blooms) was given an award also. In 1972 Nymans won thirty-five prizes at Vincent Square, of which eighteen were firsts, including the Loder Cup for an exhibit of *Rhododendron* 'Anne Rosse' (*R. sinogrande* × *R. macabeanum*). Two more fine hybrids, *Magnolia* 'Anne Rosse' (a *M. denudata* seedling, pink buds opening white), and *Sorbus* 'Leonard Messel', with mauve-tinted fruit and good autumn colour, received Awards of Merit in 1973, as did *Rhododendron cerasinum* 'Herbert Mitchell'.

One problem at Nymans that would have to be faced up to sooner or later was the age of the garden staff. In 1972 it was belatedly recognised that six of them were eligible for – indeed should already have received – the RHS's long-service medal, awarded for forty years continuous employment in one place. Cecil Nice was aged sixty-six that year; his foreman, Herbert Mitchell, was sixty-one. Three other gardeners, two of them young men, worked a full week and three more, all well over sixty, came in on a part time basis. Another, aged eighty-one, still did some light work. Anne, herself aged seventy, was most unwilling to dispense with the service of any faithful old retainer. Suggestions made by the Trust's Garden Advisers – for a new head gardener, or for a young trainee to replace Cecil Nice at some later date – fell upon stony ground: Anne was convinced that no one new could possibly feel the same devotion to herself or her beloved garden as the present staff. She confidently stated that Nice was good for eight or ten more years at least and resisted all attempts to alter the regime.

Four years later the staff situation had still not been tackled and the number of visitors, which had levelled out to around 27,000 a year, continued to compare unfavourably with the other National Trust gardens in the region. (Sheffield Park had 107,000 visitors in 1976, Sissinghurst 93,000 and Wakehurst Place 74,000). Nymans' annual financial loss had continued its inexorable rise and it was now painfully obvious that wages and other expenses would always outstrip income. The shortfall was made up each year from the Gardens Fund, but when the deficit reached £11,034 the Trust commissioned a report to see if anything could be done. Their chief finance officer toured the garden in August 1976; among his criticisms were the the indifferent quality of teas and snacks, the poor layout of the shop, which had been opened that year in what was once a wood store near the main house, rather dark and out of the way, and the general lack of directional signs. But he was unable to suggest any dramatic improvements: this time no obvious cut-back, like dispensing with the kitchen garden, presented itself. The committee could do nothing but conclude that the only way to economise would be to employ fewer men, thus entailing drastic alterations to the size and character of the garden, or else to try to increase income by encouraging more visitors and providing oppor-tunites for them to spend money. A better shop, a restaurant – or at least a proper tea-room – and a plant centre were among the suggestions.

To their great credit, the National Trust rejected the first option in favour of improving the facilities and stepping up advertising. A sum of £15,000 was set aside for building a refreshment kiosk near the entrance, to a design by Philip Jebb. This was finished in time for the beginning of the 1978 season and although it provided minimal shelter from the elements the improved supplies of tea, cakes and sandwiches were welcomed by visitors. To supplement the guide book new 'Walks' leaflets were produced, for spring and summer, and these also proved popular. Extra advertising, a television programme and various articles in the press contributed to a healthy rise in the number of visitors: 53,000 people came to Nymans in 1978. An unexpected benefaction of £8,000 was used to finance a succession of horticultural students for extra work in the garden and also provided the means to refurbish a derelict cottage in the woods. Here, in June 1978, the first Acorn Camp to be held at Nymans took place.

Another important landmark was the setting up of of the *Woody Plant Catalogue*. The National Trust, the RHS, the Royal Botanic Gardens at Kew and the Forestry Commission all agreed that some sort of central recording system for important botanical collections was eminently desirable, but they did not find it easy to unite in getting any project off the ground. Michael, with his great interest in dendrology, had often urged the Trust to make a start by drawing up lists of all the trees and shrubs growing in its gardens. Staff time and funds never seemed to be available until a grant from the Thomas Phillips Price Trust in 1978 made an initial survey possible. This was placed under the direction of the Trust's Garden Adviser (John Sales, who had taken over from Graham Stuart Thomas in 1974) and carried out by a young American biologist, Michael Zander. As a means of testing the system and assessing tree collections generally, fifty gardens were initially surveyed for conifers alone, with details of the age, measurement, provenance, etc, of the trees listed on the computer at Kew. Nymans was among this first batch of gardens and the catalogue was later extended to include all the trees here as well as in the seventeen other most important collections owned by the Trust. It was soon clear that the *Woody Plant Catalogue* provided an invaluable cross-reference system for anyone interested in dendrology, the listing of rare or endangered species being especially useful. The good work continues, now financed entirely by the National Trust, and the number of gardens covered has risen to twenty-three.

Although the National Trust had for long led the way in the preservation and maintainance of historic gardens, it did not have sufficient confidence or funds to set up any large-scale restoration schemes until the 1970s. During this decade the garden at Ham House in Surrey was restored to a seventeenth-century plan, while the early eighteenth-century landscape at Claremont, also in Surrey, cleared of its thick covering of rhododenron and laurel, revealed carefully placed garden follies and a fine grass amphitheatre. At Erddig in Clwyd the garden was refashioned to resemble a drawing of 1739, and several smaller houses had 'period' schemes designed for them. The increasing public awareness of historic gardens led to curiosity about the plants which should correctly furnish these restored layouts: some, it was believed, were already lost to cultivation. After a conference at the RHS in 1978, the National Council for the Conservation of Plants and Gardens was formed, its founder-members a small band of enthusiasts who cared more about the glories of the past than the restless search for new cultivars. Much good work is being done, but there is great anxiety in horticultural circles concerning the many plants threatened with extinction in the wild. Hybrids too (even those quite recently created) are at risk in the modern world of 'instant gardening' fostered by the garden centres, where bright colour and dwarf habit, coupled with ease of propagation and quick turnover, are of over-riding importance.

Rhododendron campylocarpum

Chapter Twelve

The Great Storm, October 1987

Oliver Messel died in July 1978. His work for the theatre had continued after the war with a large number of productions, all of which received the highest critical acclaim, in New York as well as in London. From 1950 to 1962 he was regularly employed at Glyndebourne, where John Christie had added a small private theatre to his country house. Since 1934 a short season of opera had been mounted here each year (except for a war-time break) and this was enormously influential in encouraging appreciation of something which, in England if not in Europe, has been a rather neglected art form. Oliver's enchanting sets and costumes did much to ensure Glyndebourne's increasing success and international prestige. Working there meant that he saw a great deal of Anne and Michael at Nymans (only a short drive away) and was able to introduce many stars of the theatrical and musical world to them and the garden, a tour which was an essential part of every visit.

Most of the last fifteen years of Oliver's life were spent in the West Indies, where the climate suited his health. He remodelled a house on Barbados for himself and then went on to develop a second career, designing and decorating homes, both there and on the neighbouring island of Mustique, for various friends and acquaintances who also found the lifestyle of the region most congenial.

Oliver's funeral in Barbados was attended by his nephews, Tony Snowdon and Thomas Messel, and his ashes were then brought home to Nymans. An urn on a plinth in the Wall Garden, set up by Anne, commemorates him. His water-colour of the summer border, painted many years earlier, was reproduced on the cover of a new edition of the garden guide book and has been in use ever since.

By the late 1970s both Anne and Michael Rosse were in poor health;

a hip replacement operation in 1976 had only been partially successful in relieving Anne's arthritic pain, while Michael suffered from heart and circulation problems. He had a spell in hospital in 1975 and an operation in 1978, after which he never recovered full strength. However, his chief interests were maintained until the last and at the end of June 1979 he was in London to chair a meeting of the International Dendrology Society and attend a show at Vincent Square. His many friends at these two events were sad to see him so physically depleted, and his death on 1 July, at 18 Stafford Terrace, was not unexpected. He was seventy-two.

Michael Rosse's services to the conservation movement were long and distinguished. Chairman of the Georgian Group from 1946 to 1968, he served as Deputy Chairman of the National Trust from 1970 to 1975, having been a Member of Council since 1948. He was also Chairman of the Trust's Historic Buildings Committee (after 1969 called the Properties Committee) from 1956 to 1976, and Chairman of its Gardens Panel. Apart from this work he chaired the Standing Commission on Museums and Galleries from 1956 to 1978, was Vice-Chancellor of Dublin University for fifteen years and an active member of many other learned societies, both Irish and English. Among these the International Dendrology Society (Chairman since 1964), the Garden History Society (Vice-Chairman since its foundation) and the Royal Horticultural Society (Vice-President since 1976) were perhaps closest to his heart. Under his care Birr had become one of the outstanding gardens of the British Isles, and his expert knowledge had been invaluable at Nymans.

Anne was desolated by Michael's death. Not only did she lose her dearest companion, the centre of her life, but also her place in society. The Rosse titles devolved on William, their elder son, as did the estate of Birr – henceforth Anne could go there only as a guest, not as its chatelaine. She and Michael had lived as if there were no tomorrow and William found not only that his inheritance had dwindled almost to nothing, but that his castle was in desperate need of major repairs. Ireland is a country full of roofless mansions and derelict estates, so it was a courageous act on William's part to resolve that his life would henceforth be devoted to the preservation of Birr. It meant not only that he had to give up his promising career in the United Nations, but also many other sacrifices – the Chippendale suite was among the treasures which went to pay the bills.

Anne, too, was obliged to make stringent economies. She possessed 18 Stafford Terrace in her own right and had a life-tenancy at Nymans.

For practical as well as sentimental reasons, Nymans was the best place to make a permanent base from which she could pay visits to her children and their families, but the final break up of her grandparents' London home was an eventuality she could not bear to contemplate. The Victorian Society, which she had founded there, had grown and flourished over the years. In the early 1960s it had fought to save the Euston Arch and the Coal Exchange, both in London, from demolition; sadly, both battles were lost but the furore which surrounded the campaigns did much to raise public consciousness and the tide of architectural destruction was gradually stemmed. As a direct result of the Society's efforts, such diverse monuments as the St Pancras Grand National Hotel, London, the University Museum, Oxford, and the Albert Dock, Liverpool, were saved from demolition, as well as innumerable lesser buildings. For more than twenty years Anne and Michael had supported the cause, adding Victoriana to their other abiding interests in the field of conservation and drawing much satisfaction from knowing that one of their main aims in life – the preservation of the past for the education and delight of future generations – was being increasingly realised.

Anne had hoped that a benefactor would come forward with an offer to save 18 Stafford Terrace and its contents. The National Trust were not interested in acquiring it as their Properties Committee still had an anti-Victorian bias and Anne could not offer an endowment. Friends who admired this splendid example of a late-Victorian middle-class home rallied round to help: articles appeared in the press and after much lobbying the Greater London Council agreed to purchase the house, complete with its furniture and collection of artefacts. This they did with the aid of a grant from the Land Fund (soon to be renamed the National Heritage Memorial Fund). Members of the Victorian Society volunteered to show the public round, and Linley Sambourne House was opened as a museum in the autumn of 1980.

One other asset remained to be disposed of: Lennie's splendid collection of fans. Split up and sold as individual lots these would have raised a good sum, foreign collectors being especially keen, but Anne hoped that they might be kept together somewhere in England as a lasting memorial to her father's taste and judgement. Patient negotiations ensued and the fans were finally sold to the Fitzwilliam Museum, Cambridge, in 1985, where they are now beautifully displayed in a room specially constructed for them.

Old friends who came to see Anne at Nymans found her still queen of one small kingdom. Internally the house, dim and full of treasures,

Lady Rosse with the fork and certificate presented to owners of gardens which have opened for more than forty-two years in aid of the National Gardens Scheme

its tables piled with books and *memorabilia*, retained the romantic medieval aura that Maud had loved and which Anne had so assiduously fostered. Remnants of the old life-style survived: logs from the estate kept the house warm in winter, gardeners brought in great armfuls of flowering branches to decorate the rooms in summer. The sunny courtyard garden, where a carpet of self-sown forget-me-nots was succeeded by scented herbs, roses and lilies, had scarcely changed from the private paradise of fifty years before. Beyond its high hedge the main garden was still an abiding interest and joy, around which Anne loved to walk with Cecil Nice or visiting horticultural experts, discussing past glories and future hopes. She had no wish to give up the post of Director, still feeling that she was mistress of the place and that the survival of Nymans as an historic garden, a monument to the enterprise of her father and grandfather, depended on her vigilance. But with Michael no longer there to uphold her dictates the National Trust were at last able to begin putting forward their case for radical change.

Criticisms about the standard of upkeep and lack of positive direction at Nymans had been reaching John Sales at the Gardens Adviser's office for a long time and it was clear that this was a nettle that, sooner or later, must be firmly grasped. For twenty years at least, pruning and renewal had not been sufficiently drastic for good husbandry and every winter storms took a heavy toll. When big trees – some of them grown to record size – were brought down, severe damage to the smaller growth beneath was inevitable. Clearing the debris and replanting with new stock was a stern task, more than the present staff could manage. Nymans, a shady crowded garden throughout its middle years, was sliding into an unkempt old age.

The first priority was to bring in a younger man to be Head Gardener. All attempts to persuade the Rosses to interview candidates proposed by the Trust, or to advertise the post themselves, had so far failed. By 1979 Cecil Nice had been at Nymans for more than half a century. An expert plantsman, quiet and self-effacing, he had never changed his style of management. Since the war, power tools of all kinds, fertilisers, weed killers, dozens of new labour-saving ideas, had revolutionised the way in which a large garden could be run but few of these aids had found favour at Nymans. Anything that had come to rest there – usually more by chance than design – was either already outmoded or under-used. The extensive lawns, for instance, were still cut in the old way – not by a man riding on a big machine for a few hours, but by one who spent two whole days each week walking behind an antiquated mower. A head gardener who could reorganise the work force and use modern aids skilfully, without destroying the romantic period flavour that was so much a part of Nymans, would have to be found.

Waiting in the wings was a young man cast in a very different mould from those life-long servants of traditional horticulture, James Comber and Cecil Nice. David Masters had trained as a manufacturing optician and, at the age of twenty-nine, held a good managerial post in an optics factory at Tunbridge Wells. In 1973 he decided to throw up his job and have a complete change of career. Gardening, especially the idea of garden management, appealed to him so he wrote to various bodies, the National Trust included, offering his services. As he had neither experience of garden work nor basic training, he received very dusty answers to all his enquiries. Undeterred, he sold his house, bought a caravan and set off with his wife and baby on a tour of British gardens. His self-imposed task was to learn garden management by using his eyes: analysing what made a garden beautiful, where it failed to meet its potential and what improvements might be feasible. He also asked every horticulturist he met to employ him, but without success. At the end of three months there was still no job; money was running short and a return to factory life seemed inevitable. But in the very week that he reluctantly decided to accept defeat the longed-for letter arrived: the National Trust needed a trainee gardener at Sheffield Park – would he like to come for an interview?

Archie Skinner was head gardener at Sheffield Park and David Masters spent three years there under his tutelage. But it had never been his idea to be solely a worker in the field, so, announcing that he was now fully trained, he began to make enquiries about a more responsible position – a head gardener's post, perhaps. Such audacity is rare in the gardening world but the Trust believes that managerial aspirations must be encouraged. Accordingly, in the spring of 1977 he was sent to Beningbrough Hall in Yorkshire, where refurbishment of the house was in progress and the remains of a fairly modest garden needed rescuing from decades of neglect.

Three years at Beningbrough were enough to set all straight. Another challenge, a bigger garden – preferably in the south – was what David Masters thought he would like next. He had heard that Cecil Nice at Nymans was of retirement age, so he suggested himself as a replacement. John Sales was prepared to throw all his weight behind the idea: if only Anne could be brought to agree, this unconventional self-confident new broom would be the answer to a long-standing problem. He stepped up the campaign for change at Nymans, putting forward David Masters as his preferred candidate.

Plate 10   The Lime Avenue

Plate 11 Climbing rose 'Mme Plantier' and *Rhododendron* 'Loderi' in the Wall Garden

Plate 12 The summer border

Plate 13 Clipped yews and Italian fountain in the Wall Garden

Plate 14a   Desfontainia spinosa
'Harold Comber'

Plate 14b   Berberis linearifolia
'Nymans variety'

Plate 14c   Eucryphia nymansensis
'Nymansay'

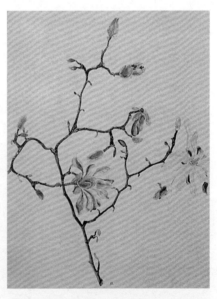

Plate 14d   Magnolia ✕ *loebneri*
'Leonard Messel'

Plate 15a　*Magnolia* 'Michael Rosse'

Plate 15b　*Magnolia* 'Anne Rosse'

Plate 15c　*Camellia* 'Maud Messel'

Plate 15d　*Camelia* 'Leonard Messel'

Plate 16　Nymans. The south front. This part of the house was gutted by fire in 1947

Plate 17   The new Rose Garden

Anne remained adamant that, as Director, she would always have the last word in the administration of the garden. Cecil Nice must stay on, but, after continuing pressure from John Sales, she eventually came round to the possibility of bringing in an assistant head gardener, who could learn from Nice and be ready to step into his shoes when the older man finally retired, perhaps in two years' time. Accordingly, David Masters arrived at Nymans in August 1980. His half-way situation was difficult at first and he found it uphill work, requiring all the tact and ingenuity he could muster, to blend into the existing team while trying to introduce some new ideas. Fortunately, years of experience on the factory floor had taught him how to manage men as well as machines and he got on well with the other staff, especially Cecil Nice, who bore no resentment but was happy to impart a lifetime's fund of horticultural knowledge to his designated successor. Within quite a short while it was accepted by all at Nymans that David Masters was in charge.

From now on, the Trust's Gardens Adviser made visits to Nymans. Graham Stuart Thomas had never felt that his advice was welcome there but John Sales and David Masters were fully in accord, so that in discussions with Anne or Cecil Nice it was their proposals which usually carried the day. A new chain-saw and a rotary mower were first on the list of tools to be acquired, while the problems of bringing the whole property into better condition were carefully assessed. Plans were drawn up for a programme of felling and replanting, and the old nursery ground was cleared of brambles and undergrowth. Fences were renewed and a number of other small but important improvements made. There were staff changes too, with more student training schemes which brought young blood into the garden. Philip Holmes, who had come to Nymans as a boy in 1970, was promoted to foreman, while Herbert Mitchell, one of the old stalwarts, continued as chief propagator. Cecil Nice, although never officially retired, was able to take things easily for the last few years of his life. He fell ill in the autumn of 1984 and died at the end of November that year, aged seventy-six.

David Masters, unlike his predecessor, had no qualms about standing up to Anne's imperious ways and she soon began to respect his opinions, as well as being grateful for his obvious commitment to the garden and the energy with which he set about improving it. Under his regime Nymans continued to exhibit regularly at Vincent Square and it was considered disappointing if fewer than twenty first prizes (and at least one cup for rhododendrons) were won in a season. Individual plants received honours also: a First Class Certificate was awarded to *Rhododendron prinophyllum* 'Philip Holmes' in 1981, an AM to *Lonicera* 'Michael Rosse' in 1982 and an FCC to *Myrtus lechleriana* (from Harold Comber seed) in 1984. Anne subscribed to Roy Lancaster's 1980 expedition to China and ninety packets of seed were sent by him to Nymans: *Hypericum maclarenii* (named for the Aberconway family) was raised in the garden and gained an Award of Merit in 1986, the first of the Lancaster plants to be so honoured.

Anne's health gradually deteriorated and after another hip replacement operation in the autumn of 1986, when she was eighty-four, her recovery was very slow. Consequently she was prepared at last to consider relinquishing the position of Director. She had hoped that her nephew Thomas Messel (son of her brother Linley's second marriage) might assume the mantle. This did not prove possible so another relative, Alistair Buchanan, offered to represent the family at Nymans. His mother, Phoebe, was the daughter of Harold, Ludwig Messel's younger son: he was thus a great-grandson of the founding genius of the garden. Phoebe's children had spent the war years at their Uncle Rudolph's home in Devon; travel was difficult then, so they hardly knew their relatives in London or the home counties. In 1954 Alistair met his second cousin Louise (daughter of 'young' Eric Parker) for the first time. They fell in love and announced their engagement in 1957. Naturally the proposed union of two separate Messel strains caused much interest in the family and Maud expressed a wish to meet the bridegroom. The young couple went to visit her at Holmsted Manor and on the same day were able to have a look at Nymans, the famous garden which Alistair had heard so much about but never seen.

Sadly, Louise's health was very fragile. She and Alistair were married in June 1959; in the autumn of 1960 her father asked Anne if they could stay at Nymans while Louise had a spell of convalescence. Alistair, like so many of Ludwig's descendants, had inherited a passion for plants and gardens; the magical beauty of Nymans at the turn of the year, coupled with a prescience that Louise had not long to live, made an indelible impression on him.

More than twenty-five years later Alistair was distressed to hear that the long association of Nymans with the Messel family might be broken. Although not a member of L. Messel & Co., he had taken over his father-in-law's role in looking after the financial affairs of various members of the family; he had, for instance, helped Anne negotiate the sales of both Stafford Terrace and the Fan Collection. He had remarried (to another Ann) and owned a house in a Wiltshire village where the garden – less than two acres in extent – had been skilfully designed for a former owner by Lanning Roper. On a steep slope, with terraces, tall clipped hedges and a swimming pool, this garden was largely formal, a finished work of art rather than a place for horticultural experiment. The thought of having some say in the management of the much more extensive – and quite different – garden at Nymans was appealing. Alistair's willingness to become involved was welcomed by the National Trust and the family were confident that with his help new life could be breathed into the garden's affairs.

Only three days after Alistair had agreed to become the family representative at Nymans, something happened which overturned all his, and the Trust's, tentative plans for the future. In the early hours of 16 October 1987 a storm of unprecedented ferocity swept over south-east England. Nymans had always been a windy garden: a big blow in the spring had brought down several trees and the staff had spent much of the summer clearing up. Thus the sound of crashing timber and the thought of more heavy work to come was enough to make everyone pull the blankets over their heads. Anne, with the wakefulness of the old, heard the wind and shuddered but David Masters, tired after a long day's work in the open air, slept soundly. He had no inkling of disaster when he awoke, but his reaction to the devastation which met his eyes when he first looked out of the window – horrified disbelief, followed by a numbed sense of shock – were feelings shared by gardeners across the region.

In just a few hours of darkness fifteen million trees had been blown down, the face of the countryside altered out of all recognition. The National Trust administered several 'areas of natural beauty' in Kent and Sussex, the counties which were worst affected. These sites were mostly ancient woodland, or high ground with fine views across well-wooded landscapes. Toy's Hill, Petts Wood and Reigate Hill were extensively damaged, although the freakishness of the wind was extraordinary, acres of woodland flattened like matchwood lying next to areas scarcely touched. Trust properties also included several fine gardens and historic parks, full of splendid mature trees: Petworth, Uppark and Knole suffered badly, but Scotney Castle, Emmetts, Sheffield Park, Wakehurst Place and Nymans were the worst hit.

For those who had tended beloved gardens for years, even lifetimes, the bereavement was cruel. At Sheffield Park Archie Skinner, head gardener for sixteen years, was so affected that his colleagues thought he might not survive the blow. At Nymans David Masters had not been in charge so long, but he too was shattered. The garden that Anne

Storm damage, October 1987. Branches torn off the cedar of Lebanon lie on the lawn. The huge up-ended root of the monkey-puzzle tree can also be seen

had known and loved all her life was now a wilderness, the labour of three generations negated. Alistair Buchanan drove over from Wilt-shire a day later expecting to see damage (he had been unable to get through to Nymans on the telephone) but was amazed by the magni-tude of the disaster. Handcross was cut off from the A23 so he had to leave his car and walk to Nymans, climbing over trees fallen across the road, but the real struggle did not begin until he approached the garden gate. From there he had to fight his way – alternately climbing and crawling – through a dense tangle of wreckage to reach the house. He found it intact, Anne safe but still trembling from shock. Together they ventured onto the one clear space of lawn that was not covered by debris. The huge old monkey-puzzle and the deodar cedar were both down, the latter perhaps the most majestic and handsome of all the trees at Nymans. The cedar of Lebanon, although badly damaged, survived, as did the copper beech, but the whole length of the pergola, wreathed with ancient wisteria, lay a hopeless tangle on the ground. Westwards, the shelter belt of yew and larch, thickly underplanted with laurels, was completely flattened, a view now opened up that had been screened from the house for more than half a century.

The National Trust put out an appeal for funds to help with clearance over the whole south-east region and volunteer groups also offered their services, but for a time the problems seemed quite overwhelming. John Sales and the gardens advisory staff, based in Cirencester, gave moral support but were not equipped to offer practical help. By great misfortune the Trust's land agent responsible for Nymans had moved to East Anglia in September and no new appointment had been made. Thus, just when co-ordination of mechanical and monetary aid was most needed (not to mention comfort and encouragement) there was no one in the area to supply it: David Masters had to set to and organise the grim task of clearing up as best he might. Hard work is the best antidote to despair and although many months of backbreaking labour – cutting logs, hauling timber, mending fences – ensued, the thought uppermost in everyone's minds was that defeat could not be contemplated. One day, Nymans would rise again.

It took some time for the National Trust to realise the extent of the disaster, but here too hope triumphed over adversity. The opportunity to replant, not piecemeal, but in a large and noble way, could be grasped with both hands. Not since before the First World War had private parks and woodlands been remodelled on a big scale: lack of money, reluctance to plan for the future, a national loss of will, meant that little had been done to enhance – or even to safeguard – the beauty of the English landscape. The storm and its aftermath made people think hard; it offered a new generation of gardeners and foresters a chance to leave their mark on the countryside, just as their ancestors had done. The National Trust, as one of the largest landowners in the country, had the knowledge and funds available to plant on a massive scale: past mistakes could be rectified, new experiments made. Sober conservation must still play a part, but now it could be accompanied by joyful creativity.

Chapter Thirteen

The Garden Reborn

In the days following the storm it was hard for anyone at Nymans to come to terms with what had happened, but as always after any major disaster, a spirit of camaraderie quickly developed. First priority was to work out how best to manage without modern communications. Power lines were down, telephones cut, paths, roads and railways blocked by fallen timber. The main transport arteries were reopened fairly quickly, but other services were very slow; people who lived down country lanes had to wait, in some places for several weeks, before wheeled traffic reached them or their power lines were reinstated.

David Masters rallied his gardeners: the drives and paths had to be cleared, then they could see what might be saved from the rest of the wreckage. On the north side of the garden the Pinetum had taken the full force of the wind and was almost clear-felled, the huge conifers crushing masses of rhododendrons and smaller trees as they came down. The Californian redwood and the Wellingtonia, both giant trees, survived; so did the much younger dawn redwood, planted soon after this species, hitherto known only from fossils, had been discovered growing in China in 1941. The lime avenue at the bottom of the Pinetum meadow also escaped almost intact, but of the twenty-eight champion trees for which the garden was renowned twenty were destroyed. The Top Garden suffered less, the fine large *Meliosma veitchiorum* (grown from Wilson seed) and the *Nothofavus menziesii* surviving, as well as most of the magnolias. The Wall Garden had, as always, provided good protection, but even here two rare *Nothofagus* species, *N. fusca* and *N. solanderi*, the largest of their kind in Britain, were lost.

Once the first shocks had been assimilated there was room for optimism. Nymans had been a garden overfilled with trees, many of which had already passed their prime, so it would now be possible to take a fresh look at various long-standing problems. Alistair Buchanan

The team responsible for clearing the storm damage, 1987–8. *Standing, left to right*: Floyd Summerhayes, Robin Masson. *Seated*: Philip Holmes (foreman) David Masters (Head Gardener), Tony Locker Lampson

had to face the fact that his new job was not to be caretaker of an established garden, a pleasant part-time interest, lightly undertaken, but a much more demanding venture: helping to plan and oversee the birth of a new one. If the National Trust would throw all its resources into the challenge, if David Masters and his garden staff could battle through the arduous task of clearing up, courage and enthusiasm would surely carry the day. Everyone must set their sights on the ultimate reward: a revitalised and beautiful garden, even better – if that were possible – than the old one in its prime.

The last RHS Show of 1987 fell on 24 November. Determined to show that triumph was possible even in adversity, David Masters planned to stage a spectacular exhibit. In 1980 Anne had presented the RHS with the Rosse Cup in memory of Michael; this was awarded annually to three vases of conifers, shown for their foliage. Nymans had won the cup in 1982 and 1986 and would enter and win again, but something on a bigger scale was now possible: branches could be cut from the prostrate trunks of trees whose best foliage had previously been inaccessible. The result was a most impressive array. David Masters received many congratulations, as his stand of forty-nine vases brought Nymans the first Gold Medal it had ever won in an open competition at Vincent Square.

Freshly cut material was not only suitable for exhibition but had a much more important practical use – the *Woody Plant Catalogue* was about to prove its value. Immediately after the storm John Sales contacted Michael Lear, now in charge of the project, and commissioned him to establish what losses had been incurred: he was then to devise an emergency propagation programme for all the Trust's afflicted gardens. Various nurseries which specialised in modern propagating techniques were contacted, cuttings were quickly dispatched, and the precise genetic stock of 60 per cent of all the stricken trees was saved for posterity. Not only Trust gardens but also some privately-owned ones, such as Borde Hill, were to benefit from this major operation.

It was decided to hold an Open Day at Nymans on 10 January 1988 to allow the public to see the extent of the damage. A great deal of work had already been done, but the 3,700 visitors who arrived that day still found something which bore more resemblance to a savage wilderness than to a garden. By trial and error David Masters had worked out the most effective methods of clearing the ground, and such good progress was made that the garden was able to open at the usual time – Easter – with the major part of the work completed.

Visitors by the north drive on the open day, 10 January 1988

Fortunately many of the rhododendrons, although severely damaged, did survive, breaking anew from stumps. Some of the smaller trees were successfully winched upright, but approximately 490 large ones had been lost; their roots had all to be dug out and burned, a mammoth task.

Much thought was given by all parties concerned as to what the planting priorities should be at Nymans. On some matters agreement was easy: the shelter belts must be replaced as quickly as possible, some specimen trees planted to replace those lost from the lawn, and of course the Pinetum should be recreated as a garden bereft of stately conifers – the earliest of the Messel passions – was unthinkable. Various long-term projects had been discussed before the storm but, with money coming in from the disaster fund, a grant expected from English Heritage, and strong support from the gardens advisory team, more radical changes were now possible.

John Sales, David Masters and Alistair Buchanan began to draw up lists and discuss plans. The problems of visitor access and circulation, always acute at Nymans, could be addressed. Some of the paths must be realigned to make a better route through the garden, and new drainage (an expensive exercise, too long deferred) was essential.

Surfaces, steps and edgings must also be upgraded. Inevitably some schemes already in train had to be postponed for a year or two, but it was agreed that the summer border in the Wall Garden should be as fine a spectacle as ever. The familiar annual tasks of sowing seed, potting up and planting out provided staff with welcome relief from the heavy clearance work, which continued unremittingly throughout 1988.

On 14 May 1988 the family held a party on the lawn. Anne, now aged eight-six and very frail, came out of the house to perform a symbolic gesture, the planting of a young monkey-puzzle tree. This was set just where the old one had been, with many hopes that it would provide as noble a spectacle for the descendants of the planter as its forebear had for her father and grandfather. For the task Anne used a spade presented by her son Tony and her nephew Thomas Messel, its blade and handle inscribed with her name and the date.

Extensive replanting began in earnest that autumn. David Masters hoped to involve local residents more closely in the garden's renaissance, so he planned a special tree-planting day for the children of Handcross Primary School. The area just north of the Wall Garden (originally filled with a mixture of Norway spruce, beech and chestnut) had been completely flattened; as this was an important windbreak, its early reinstatement was essential. Planting holes were prepared and a stock of young sweet chestnut trees laid in. When fifty-three children arrived on 14 October, a year almost to the day from when the hurricane struck, David told them about the garden and then gave out tools. Everyone set to work digging and planting with the greatest enthusiasm. Once the trees were in the ground handfuls of bluebell seed were distributed. Each child sowed his or her own patch, making a place to which they might return with pleasure, David hoped, all through their lives.

Other more sophisticated parties took place. On 31 October the Handcross Women's Institute planted a cedar of Lebanon on the lawn. Although the old cedar might survive a few more storms, it was reaching the end of its natural span and it seemed wise to have a replacement ready. The deodar cedar with its beautiful drooping foliage, whose loss had caused David Masters more regret than that of any other tree in the garden, was a feature which had to be reinstated. Its planting was, rightly, the head gardener's privilege: as David firmed the ground around the waist-high plant, he gave it strict instructions not to die.

The replanting of the Rose Garden, for which John Sales and his assistant, Isabelle van Groeningen, had already drawn up plans, was not

Children from Handcross Primary School planting trees, one year after the storm, 14 October 1988

able to go ahead that winter as no staff time could be spared. But here at least the storm had done some good: previously a shady spot, never ideal for growing roses, it was now deprived of tree cover and promised to be a far better site. The design was redrawn with this in mind, and 115 different varieties of the old-fashioned roses that Maud had loved so much were accommodated. New metal arches and obelisks were erected, ready to take the weight of climbers and ramblers whose vigour was well known. It was decided that the old concrete well-head in the centre should be replaced by a new fountain and Vivian ap Rhys Price was commissioned to design one in bronze. Planting was done in the winter of 1988/9, and so splendid is the soil at Nymans that growth exceeded all expectation, the roses flowering magnificently in their very first season.

Meanwhile the same design team was hard at work on a much larger project, the new Pinetum. Michael Lear's propagating scheme had been a great success and the infant trees derived from many of the old Nymans giants were already growing lustily, although they were not yet large enough to be set out in the open. Other cultivars were needed and Muriel's list in *A Garden Flora* was consulted. Lawsons cypress, which comes in a great number of variations, was a Messel favourite:

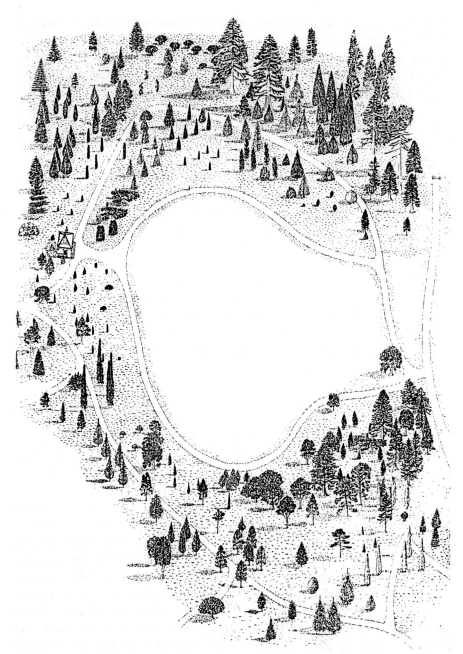

Plan of the new Pinetum designed by John Sales and Isabelle van Groeningen. Drawn for the National Trust by C. Renow-Clarke

fortunately, cuttings from the great collection at Bedgebury Pinetum had been taken before the storm and these too were nearly ready for planting out. Some of the other varieties required were donated by nurseries up and down the country (the Savill Garden being particularly generous), and altogether 284 plants of 147 varieties were assembled. These were set out in a piece of ground behind the potting sheds so that everything would be ready by the time the grand scheme was finally approved. Planting was all done, in one great burst of activity, during April 1990.

Apart from the loss of the old Pinetum, the most noticeable and grievous change at Nymans was in the area south-east of the house. Here, falling trees had caused so much damage to the Laurel Walk and its surroundings that a tough decision was made: almost everything still standing in this part of the garden would have to be cleared away. The resulting naked area was painful to behold (the back of the Italian loggia, never before in view, looked especially vulnerable), so the work of replanting went forward as quickly as possible. The old long, straight Laurel Walk – an important contrasting feature in a garden which was otherwise so informal – was reinstated, but instead of the old mixed planting of aucuba, cherry laurel, holly and yew, only cherry laurel (*Prunus laurocerasus*) was chosen, for its uniformity and ease of maintenance. In time this would grow into a dense screen, to recreate the dark mysterious pathway along which generations of Messel children had learnt to bicycle.

Nature graciously refrained from hampering the workers during the first two winters of clearing and replanting, the weather being neither too cold nor too wet to prevent good progress. The garden staff were worried that the loss of tree cover would lead to fatal chilling of the smaller plants; however, it was not cold, but drought, which was to prove the greatest hazard. In 1989 no rain fell – other than two showers – from 28 April to 14 September. Hose bans were soon in operation throughout the southern counties and the new planting, representing an enormous outlay of money, time and effort, was at risk. Valuable old stock, too, such as the Himalayan rhododendrons, originally planted beneath groves of trees to simulate their natural cool, damp habitat, suffered badly. The gardeners found carrying cans of water all summer long no joke: each plant was strictly rationed, the weakest coddled with an extra cupful only if its condition looked desperate. Irrigation had always been a problem to Nymans – water-flow to the three outlets in the garden was so poor that only one tap could be used at a time – so David Masters had to improvise: an old enamel bath loaded onto a trailer caused onlookers much amusement, but by this means precious fluid was transported to the plants which most needed it. The following summer was almost as dry (no rain from 1 July to 29 September) and even hotter, the thermometer registering 97 °F on 4 August.

Visitor numbers fell away the first couple of years after the storm, as word had got round that nothing worth seeing was left at Nymans. But for those in the know there was plenty to admire, and the feelings of hope and excitement as the new garden gradually took shape were palpable. By the spring of the 1990 it was clear to everyone that a magnificent recovery was being staged, and visitors began to return in large numbers. Most parts of the garden were again a pleasure to visit, with the magnolias, camellias and rhododendrons as splendid as ever in the spring, the Heath Garden and the summer border a blaze of colour. The new Rose Garden made a splendid showing, and a ceremonial opening was performed on 29 June.

Although old friends still mourned the loss of the fine trees, the shaded walks and the dense thickets of holly and rhododendron which had made Nymans such a 'Sleeping Beauty' garden, no thinking person

Alistair Buchanan, at the opening of the new Rose Garden, 29 June 1990. Lady Frances Armstrong-Jones is about to cut the ribbon

could deny that some changes had been long overdue. Once the new framework was finally in place, luxuriant growth, always Nymans hallmark, would soon soften the harsh corners.

The orgy of replanting was of course backed by very careful thought. Nymans had reached a peak of eminence because of its historic and well-documented plant collections, the upkeep and enhancement of which must continue to be of the very first importance. Over the years, planting throughout the garden had become somewhat muddled, and rather than continue the old policy of filling gaps with whatever came most easily to hand, a clear strategy for the future would have to be worked out. Nymans is a much more loosely constructed garden than Hidcote or Sissinghurst, its component parts larger and more strikingly different one from the other. This was a virtue that could be emphasised in various ways. Concentrated grouping of the flora from distinct areas of the world, with emphasis on the famous collectors especially associated with Nymans, seemed the best option. Such an arrangement would be of great interest to a public gradually being made aware of the vital role played by cultivated plants in a world of shrinking resources.

The Americas, both North and South, were well represented in the Pinetum, as well as in the arboretum across the park, where autumn-colouring trees showed up well. The Top Garden still retained several fine old trees grown direct from Wilson seed and was especially rich in Asiatic magnolias and their hybrids. In the Wall Garden the larger Chinese and Himalayan shrubs grew well and there was room now for more of these to be accommodated. Harold Comber's work with southern hemisphere plants was of special relevance at Nymans, so it was decided to devote a significant area around the perimeter of the Wall Garden to his collection. Although a few original Comber plants still grew here, some more were gathered together from other parts of the garden to make a 'Chilean border'. Seed brought back from South America by Martin Gardiner and Sabina Knees, who had been there on a collecting trip in 1986–7, helped fill in any gaps. Sun-lovers of any provenance would be accommodated, as before, in the Rock and Heath gardens, where pieris and many of the smaller species of rhododendron, collected by Forrest, Kingdon-Ward and Rock, also flourished. The planting on the main lawn would continue to reflect the Victorian 'gardenesque' design, with a few fine specimen trees surrounded by loosely-shaped beds of rhododendrons and azaleas.

Five years after the storm the urgent pace of planning and replanting could be allowed to slacken, but a gardener's work is never done. 'Fine

The Laurel Walk: new plants by the ruins. The damaged beech tree was later felled

tuning' of the whole design must be the next priority, together with sympathetic control of the exuberant new growth. The last few years have allowed little time for breeding or for showing, but several new cultivars raised a decade or so ago are showing great promise: a sorbus and a magnolia, both named for Cecil Nice, are awaiting their turn to go to Vincent Square. Another fine magnolia, of unknown parentage, had grown at Nymans for more years than anyone could remember. Slow to mature, it had never been exhibited, but David Masters, confident that here was a worthy memorial to Nymans' first head gardener, named it 'James Comber'. Sadly, the tree fell victim to the storm, but David took cuttings which grew away well, although it will be many years before flowering branches can be picked for showing.

Since 1979 William Rosse had carried on his father's work at Birr, beautifying the grounds, planting rare trees, sponsoring plant-hunting expeditions and exchanging plants and seeds with Nymans. The hope that wild sources can continue to provide good new plants is fading fast, but there is still no limit to the possibilities offered by hybridisation. Here Nymans will continue to play an important part as it was always the principal aim of the Messels, and later the National Trust, to produce plants of garden value. It was in the development and selection of such plants that Nymans had become most famous, so increased attention to such matters, and a return to regular attendance at the RHS shows, will see the garden once again established in the top league of horticultural excellence.

A large part of the National Trust's income depends on membership and visitor numbers. Amenities for the public scarcely existed at Nymans and once the new planting was complete it was more necessary than ever to consider the needs of visitors. There had always been underlying differences of opinion as to how the estate should best be managed and Anne's death in July 1992, after a long but peaceful decline, was another turning point in the history of the garden. It was a sad day when the old Nymans lost its fiercest protector but so much had altered since the storm that even she might have conceded that more major changes were inevitable. The Trust, with Alistair's support, began a radical reappraisal of the whole property. Funds were at last forthcoming and a new entrance kiosk, a large shop and a tea room (designed by Robert Adam in marquee style) were all built at the northern entrance and opened in 1995. An extended picnic area and enclosure for plant sales completed the transformation. The effect on visitor numbers was dramatic. Suddenly

Nymans found itself in the limelight and almost at once became one of the National Trust's most popular garden destinations.

The rise in gate money was welcomed by the Trust but a garden is a fragile environment; lawns, paths and plants all suffer if there is overcrowding. New pathways into the garden were devised to spread the load, one leading to the Pinetum and the wild flower meadow and the other through banks of hydrangea 'Blue Wave' into the Top Garden. This area was greatly improved when the early summer border, with its loose arrangement of flowering shrubs and clumps of cottage garden flowers, was repeated on the opposite side of the path. The most obtrusive of the old greenhouses was demolished and the mixture of half-hardy perennials in its place come into bloom when the adjacent Rose Garden has passed its peak. Further on the path again divides, one route leading into the Wall Garden and the other downhill to the Lime Avenue, past a new plantation of fifteen Davidia involucrata. When grown to flowering size this grove of 'handkerchief trees' will make the kind of dramatic statement for which the founder of the garden was renowned.

To the delight of walkers and the local community, the extensive woodland on the eastern side of the estate is now accessible. Clearance of dead wood and rubbish in the 250 acres was a major effort but the results have been well worth while. A path from the south-east corner of the main garden leads across the park to the arboretum, where several fine old trees survived the storm and young ones have been planted for autumn colour. From here three signposted paths wind down through dense woodland to the lakeside. The trees are mostly native oak, beech and hazel but groups of redwoods, cedars and firs were planted here in 1910. Several of these have grown very large and one Wellingtonia is close to being the tallest tree in Sussex. Mosses, fungi and all sorts of insects flourish and in spring wood anemones and sheets of bluebells in the clearings make this another kind of paradise, quite different from the manicured garden on the hilltop. Paths continue down towards the lake which has been cleaned and restocked. An unexpected discovery was that the stream which feeds it runs through a series of pools and mini-cascades. These were constructed in the 1920s but the project was abandoned after only a few years and quite forgotten since. Now cleared and repaired this delightful 'water garden' attracts an abundance of wild life.

On the other side of the estate is an area known as the Wild Garden. During the 1920s this had been the home of shrubs and trees for which no room could be found elsewhere. Most of these did not survive for long and clearance has recently taken place with much new planting. As the ground is comparatively level the average walker finds the paths less daunting than those on the vertiginous slopes of the main woodland. This is a delightful place to stroll round appreciating all the wild flowers, butterflies and birds that are so threatened by the ever-increasing urbanisation of our cherished landscape.

Perhaps the most exciting development for Nymans devotees has been the opening of the house to visitors. Anne had inhabited only a small part of the old building (which was becoming more dilapidated every year) and her death left the Trust with a problem. Another big injection of cash would be needed to set the house to rights. From a financial point of view the best course might be to lease the house to a wealthy tenant, someone prepared to do the necessary repairs in exchange for the chance to live in such a beautiful environment. Fortunately for those who love family history, this plan was not followed. Instead the Trust shouldered the burden and after extensive refurbishment visitors were able in 1997 to have limited access to the ground floor where the Garden Hall, Library and Dining Room are now on view. Low ceilinged and dimly lit, these rooms are furnished exactly as they were in Anne's time. Here she passed the evening of her life, surrounded by photographs and beloved mementos of three generations of the Messel family.

From the house one can step into the courtyard garden, surrounded by a high wall. Access to the courtyard was formerly denied to visitors who always longed to look inside. The family loved the simple formal layout here and spent many peaceful summer afternoons sitting in the sun. It is still an oasis of calm, a wonderful contrast to the rest of the garden which has lush extravagance as its keynote. Nymans holds one more secret – what lies behind the dramatic centrepiece of the estate, the tall Gothic façade with its blanked-out windows? Some argue that this romantic ruin

The Library

should remain untouched but Alistair's long-cherished plan is to plant tender shrubs and climbers inside the roofless space, making magic gardens in the former Great Hall and Drawing Room for visitors to wonder at, or even walk through. However the expenditure necessary to stabilise the crumbling walls means that it may be some time before this idea can be realised.

Since 1890 Nymans has been the heart and home of the Messel family. During the last fifty years it has continued as the focus for an ever-growing cousinage, a meeting point for all those bonded to the place by feelings of affection, sentiment and pride. Seeing the life work of their forebears honoured in the Trust's faithful restructuring of the garden has given cause for gratitude and satisfaction. Not just in specialist circles but among a host of garden lovers the name of Messel is recognised as one that has played a significant part in bringing beauty and variety to the English scene. Nymans today is a living memorial to all who laboured there and love it dearly: their greatest hope is that others may draw pleasure, comfort and inspiration from its beauties.

Dipelta ventricosa

Bibliography and Sources

Published works
(the place of publication is London unless otherwise stated)

Castle, C., *Oliver Messel*, Thames and Hudson, 1986.

Clapham, A.R., *The Oxford Book of Trees*, Oxford University Press, 1975.

Coats, A., *Garden Shrubs and Their Histories*, Vista Books, 1963.

Fletcher, H., *The Story of the Royal Horticultural Society 1804–1968*, Oxford University Press, 1969.

Gaze, J., *Figures in a Landscape: a History of the National Trust*, Barrie and Jenkins, 1988.

The Hillier Manual of Trees and Shrubs, Winchester, Hillier Nurseries, 1972.

Kingdon-Ward, F., *Plant Hunting on the Edge of the World*, Gollancz, 1930.

Lees-Milne, J., *Ancestral Voices*, Chatto and Windus, 1975.

Lucas Phillips, C.E., & Barber, P., *The Rothschild Rhododendrons*, Exbury Gardens, 1987.

Messel, L., *A Garden Flora. Trees and Flowers Grown in the Gardens at Nymans 1890–1915*; illustrations by Alfred Parsons, foreword by William Robinson; notes by Muriel Messel; *Country Life*, 1918.

Robinson, W., *The English Flower Garden*, John Murray, 1883.

The Royal Horticultural Society Gardeners Encyclopedia of Plants and Flowers, C. Brickell (ed.), Dorling Kindersley, 1989.

Street, F., *Rhododendrons*, Cassel & Co., 1965.

Thomas, G.S., *Gardens of the National Trust*, Weidenfeld and Nicolson, 1979.

Wilson, E., *A Naturalist in Western China*, Methuen, 1913.

Wright, T., *The Gardens of Britain: Kent, Sussex and Surrey*, Batsford, 1978.

Periodicals

Country Life
The Garden
Gardeners' Chronicle
Garden Life
The Journal of the Royal Horticultural Society
Kew Bulletin

Unpublished diaries and letters

Diaries of Marion Sambourne and letters of Maud Messel (Victorian
    Society/Royal Borough of Kensington and Chelsea)
Letters of Leonora Messel (Judith Hiller)

Index

References to photographs and illustrations are in *italics*.